Goal

My Journey From Afghanistan

by

Mohammad B. Alikhail

Goal
My Journey From Afghanistan

Copyright © 2008 by Mohammad B. Alikhail

All rights reserved. No part of this book may be used or reproduced by any means, graphic, electronic, or mechanical, including photocopying, recording, taping or by any information storage retrieval system without the written permission of the publisher except in the case of brief quotations embodied in critical articles and reviews.

The views expressed in this work are solely those of the author and do not necessarily reflect the views of the publisher, and the publisher hereby disclaims any responsibility for them.

iUniverse books may be ordered through booksellers or by contacting:

iUniverse
1663 Liberty Drive
Bloomington, IN 47403
www.iuniverse.com
1-800-Authors (1-800-288-4677)

Because of the dynamic nature of the Internet, any Web addresses or links contained in this book may have changed since publication and may no longer be valid. The views expressed in this work are solely those of the author and do not necessarily reflect the views of the publisher, and the publisher hereby disclaims any responsibility for them.

ISBN: 978-0-595-47048-8 (pbk)
ISBN: 978-0-595-91330-5 (ebk)
ISBN: 978-1-4401-0626-2 (cloth)

Printed in the United States of America

For the people of Afghanistan

Table of Contents

Preface ix
Acknowledgments xiii
Chapter One: Bad-bakht (The Unlucky One) 1
Chapter Two: A Boy's Promise to Become Literate 7
Chapter Three: Dying Trees 19
Chapter Four: Trapped Birds 29
Chapter Five: Faded and Unraveled 35
Chapter Six: Pulse Rate 49
Chapter Seven: Nightfall 63
Chapter Eight: Testing Culture 71
Chapter Nine: Between the Lines 83
Chapter Ten: The Rewards of Patriotism 91
Chapter Eleven: Fighting for Breath 103
Chapter Twelve: Connections 113
Chapter Thirteen: Word 123
Chapter Fourteen: Options 137
Chapter Fifteen: Deep Roots and a New Leaf 151
Chapter Sixteen: Nametags and Timecards 163
Chapter Seventeen: Almost Impossible 179
Afterword 191

Preface

Every soul holds a dream. My soul has held many. I've strived to achieve dream after dream until I arrived here, in front of the very desk at which I sit. After everything I've been through, my soul holds yet another dream. That is why I am holding a tape recorder in my hand.

I decided to dictate the story of my life and journey from Afghanistan to the United States so I might make some difference in the world. I hope these recollections will inspire readers to look at their own souls' dreams with renewed vigor.

Perhaps readers will see more than their own dreams. Perhaps they will look upon others, especially those who appear to be strangers, as souls not too different from themselves, that is, as souls who hold dreams and are worthy of achieving them.

All too often, we are not seen as the unique individuals that we are. Rather, too many people see cutouts. Upon looking at those of us who come from faraway lands, many people stamp us as "foreign" and look to the next face and then the next until they find someone to whom they can relate. I want to help people all over the world, especially those who live in Western countries (which is where most people from Third World countries migrate for job opportunities and professional training) understand more about the foreign faces who live and breathe among them.

The world is suffering. Thoughts and feelings of difference and indifference separate people who come from various neighborhoods, nations, and notions. These divisions make acts of aggression and war acceptable. But if we were to recognize each other as similar beings with similar sentiments, then we'd regard such acts against complete strangers from around the world as unacceptable. It would be as unacceptable as such acts against our dearest family members. Then some of the suffering would subside.

If you have ever longed for something, been afraid to go after it, disregarded cautionary internal whispers, or pounced on opportunity, then you can relate to me and many more like me. We foreigners are so much more than our labels.

Some of us are educated; some of us are not. Through the years that I have lived in the United States, many of my friends have told me that they think foreign graduates, specifically foreign medical graduates, come from very wealthy families. They are wrong.

"How else could such a fortunate dream come true?" they ask me. People all over the world decide to leave behind the countries in which they were born—as well as their families, jobs, and hobbies—in search of a new and better life, which is usually in the more prosperous Western countries.

I left my home country—along with everything and everyone I knew—to build a better life. So did many of my childhood friends and classmates who were studying medicine at the University of Kabul in Kabul, Afghanistan. We left because we were tired of enduring everything in exchange for nothing. We decided to risk life itself for a life of hope.

Our travels to the West were a series of long and dangerous trips that called for many risks and decisions that we often had to make within a split second. Some of us reached our goal. Some did not. Some gave up or became the victims of exploitation and death en route to our dreams.

My travels and adventures eventually led me to the United States, but the journey did not end there. The real journey began after the travel. My travel to the West was a test of body and mind. My journey in the West is a test of fire to my soul.

Not only do I hope that this book will open readers' eyes to their own worthiness and the worthiness of their dreams, I hope it will open them to the similarities that bind us, including the prosperous, the poor, the Jewish, the Christian, and the Muslim. Maybe, if we'd just step over the chasm of man-made labels that divide us, we'd be able to look each other in the eyes and see each other as the beings of worth that we are. We'd then put faces, hearts, and dreams to the label; see each other as brothers; and work out solutions that are above the aggression and apathy to which we resort.

Even with all of the advances in science and technology that our world has made, the twenty-first century is a dangerous time to live. Despite our material heights, we tread a world of spiritual lows, a world that lacks peace. I sincerely hope and pray that something I say in this book will somehow contribute to the endeavors toward peace for the sake of all of us, our children, and all future generations. Thank you for embarking on my journey with me.

Acknowledgments

I would like to thank and show my greatest appreciation to the people who made it possible for me to write this book.

The first person is Murray Logan, my boss at the University of British Columbia in Canada. He is the first person who encouraged me to write about my journey from Afghanistan.

I'd also like to thank Dr. Benjamin Wilson. I met him while he worked as a resident in the Anderson Family Practice Residency Program in Anderson, South Carolina. He came to know the stories of my journey during his rotations in internal medicine. He told me that he had written some news articles in the past and was willing to start my book for me. He asked me questions, and I answered them into a tape recorder. By the end of his three-year residency, we had finished a rough copy of the book.

The person who most helped me believe that my story could be shaped into a book is Emily Keller. She helped me with the book and offered emotional support as I revisited the details of my past. My gratitude to her cannot be expressed in words.

I'd also like to thank Linda Jay Geldens for her copyediting services. She caught errors and offered valuable clarity to my work.

Dr. Harry Morse, Julie Morse, and their daughter, Elizabeth Morse, who named the book, also deserve recognition. Their help and support means the world to me.

Finally, I'd like to thank my beautiful wife and my wonderful children, who keep me going on a daily basis. I am not sure where I'd be without them.

"Are you going to call it?" the nurse asks, pressing the heels of her hands into the dead woman's chest.

Mohammad Alikhail

The body is blue and cold. The woman, whose body has been found in a North Pacific river earlier that day, looks dead.

"Get me some bretylium," I order.

"What?" the other nurse asks.

Chapter One:
Bad-bakht (The Unlucky One)

I whispered the request to Mother. It was just loud enough to interrupt the group of women who chatted between sips of tea. I wasn't certain if I had managed to capture everyone's attention, but Mother's response confirmed it. All at once, ten small porcelain cups clinked in their saucers as the women stopped sipping and held their tongues. Mother, the fair-skinned hostess, was blushing. The cats were curious.

"Darling," Mother said, reaching with her right hand into her pocket. The palm of her left hand rose to my face and cupped my chin. "Here."

I felt her plump fingers stiffen subtly. For a moment, her eyes flashed with anger. Fear's lightning response struck my gut. Just then, her lips parted into a smile as her eyes and hand softened.

"Five rupees?" she asked, withdrawing her hand from her pocket. "Here they are. Now run along and play, my dear."

Her last words merged with a soft laugh as she looked around at her guests and raised her teacup to her lips. The gossiping cats were satisfied. They relaxed their ears and resumed the consumption of dark tea and light gossip. Mother turned to me. Her eyes locked with mine. They held me in their gaze.

"Thank you, Mother," I said, prying my ten-year-old body from the magnetic force that held it. I turned around and walked out the door.

* * *

A handful of sweets later, I returned home. The cats and their judgments were gone. But Mother was still there.

"Mohammad!" she yelled, grabbing my ear.

My candy fell to the floor.

"Ouch! Ouch! Stop!" I whined and protested.

"What were you thinking?" she asked.

She dragged me over to the kitchen area, where she was cooking. She couldn't afford not to multitask, not even while scolding me.

"What?" I asked.

"What?" she repeated. "Oh, you, you *Bad-bakht*, you know what!" She picked up a knife and pointed it at my nose. "Don't you ever—*ever*—take advantage of me in front of my friends again! Do you hear me?"

"Yes," I said.

My ear burned in its twisted shape.

"Promise?" she asked.

She twisted my ear even further and pulled my head toward her. Her eyes were as brown as molasses. They poured into mine as she looked down at me. I felt her embarrassment, and I was sorry to have caused it.

"Okay. I promise," I said.

She let go of my ear and lowered the knife. I softened up to her as she picked up an onion from the small mound that sat on the old wooden table.

Chop! Chop! Chop!

I pressed into her side and inhaled her aroma.

"I won't do it again," I said.

* * *

I lied. I did it again and again. Sometimes, it was even worse.

There were times when my trick didn't work because my mother was out of the rupees that usually jingled within her pockets. Rather than give up, I'd let out a big sigh and drop my head in disappointment.

"You really can't give me the money?" I'd ask. After a few seconds of staring at the floor, I'd turn the saddest eyes I could possibly manage toward her and add, "Really?"

Eventually, one of Mother's friends would rescue her from the embarrassment.

"Hey, child," she'd say. " Don't be so sad. Here, I'll give you the rupees your mother owes you."

"No, you don't need to—" Mother would start, but she would never finish.

"Really, it's no problem," her friend would say.

I'd smile and say, "Thank you."

I would avoid Mother's eyes altogether. But I'd still feel them staring at me.

I'll never forget those eyes. They were like the sea in temperament. When she wasn't mad, Mother had the kindest and calmest eyes I have ever known. I sought their warmth, love, and knowing looks. I sought to stare at her eyes in the same way that man seeks to reach the point where land ends and ocean begins. It is the point where he can stare off into the horizon and feel everything he needs at once. In one look, her eyes told me what some mothers take an evening of holding and sharing to convey. No matter what was going on, I could look up at her soft face and know that everything was going to be okay…except, of course, when I was being naughty.

* * *

Chop! Chop! Chop!

"*Bad-bakht.*"

It means "unlucky one." It's what she's always called me for the circumstances of my birth. She paused for a moment and looked at me.

"What am I going to do with you?" she asked. She sighed, shook her head, and returned her attention to the half piece of onion on the cutting table. "You'd better go pick up your candy before someone else gets it."

Mother didn't dwell on one misbehaving child for too long. She had too much to do.

* * *

Every day, Mother was the first one up and the last one to go to bed. No matter how little sleep she had gotten, she was always ready to accomplish the next task, which usually involved the preparation of food. Her short, medium-sized frame and dark hair carried the scent of onions and a bouquet of spices, including cardamom, cumin, and curry. She was an excellent cook. The local villagers considered it an honor when she made kabobs and *pialu* rice, a traditional Afghan dish of sugar, oil, and cumin, for their special occasions.

Mother rose every morning at four o'clock and tiptoed to the kitchen. From there, she lit her stove and forced the darkness that had blinded, but not hindered, her to retreat. She sometimes stood by the stove and warmed her hands. Most of the time, she didn't hesitate between tasks. Her work flowed like a ballet.

She had a way with fire. Fire longed to burn for her. Even during rain and wind, fire rose and danced with her. And, once a fire came to life, it held on tenaciously until every last drop of fuel and fiber of wood had been spent. I loved to watch her work with fire during the day, but the morning fire was the only one that belonged to her and her alone.

After Mother lit the morning stove, she set the teapot on the fire and turned her heart to God. After her prayers, she set her sights on the day's meals, which required peeling and chopping vegetables hours in advance.

Though she started cooking long before the sun came up, she was always the last one to eat. And magically—in the way that only mothers know—for whatever was left for her, she smiled with satisfaction. And then, for the fifth time that day, just before she finally turned to her bed, she turned her heart to God.

Her way with prayer was like her way with fire. It was quiet and alone, as if everyone around her was still locked in slumber. She never prostrated herself for show, as I had seen many people do. Nor did she talk about prayer, the Koran, and what people ought to do. Rather, she lived her life by example. While the women in my family followed her guidance closely, the men did not.

Meal preparation was only one of the many tasks Mother had to oversee in a home occupied by twenty-one people, which mostly included children. She and Father had five boys and one girl. Father and his second wife, whom I referred to as my stepmother, had three boys and two girls. In addition to our fourteen family members, my uncle and his six children also lived with us. Mother took care of the children, washed most of the laundry, and oversaw the chores. She never complained about the long days of work that usually kept her busy until eleven o'clock at night or of the nights that the cries and complaints of children often interrupted.

Mother was generous, patient, kind, and always ready to listen. The same traits that helped her accomplish day after day of hard work with effortless grace endeared her to everyone in our village except, of course, to one person. A mutual, tangible dislike sat like an elephant between Mother and Father's second bride, Miriam.

* * *

On March 18, 1961, Mother was one of many women around the world who were wrapped up in labor. She was one of many women who breathed, pushed, and delivered a new life into the world. She was one of thousands of women who looked into the eyes of her newborn child and cried. She cried in joy, and she cried in pain. But the pain was not from labor.

Mother was a pro at laboring. She was the midwife of her village. With an ever-available shoulder, she was everybody's mother. She was the one for whom women sent when they themselves went into labor.

Ironically, the comforter delivered her fifth son in solitude. Then she wondered if her husband's new bride was as beautiful as she once had been.

"Here he is," Mother said.

She cradled my slight frame onto her chest and said, "*Bad-bakht.*"

From that day on, though she loved and sheltered me, whenever I slipped and messed up or whenever she was stressed and angry, I was "*Bad-bakht.*" No matter what I did, Mother never forgot that the day of my birth was the day that Father turned his affections toward a younger wife. Mother was twenty years old.

* * *

My name is Mohammad Bahadur Alikhail, and this is my story. My life began in Saikanda, Afghanistan. Father also started life in the "Land of Afghans," a country that was long ago a hub of trade and migration.

Chapter Two:
A Boy's Promise to Become Literate

"Daddy! Daddy!" the four-year-old boy yelled as he ran up to his father.

Tall for his age, the boy was also slender. He had dark skin, and his bright eyes always sparkled, especially when he was hopeful of reaching his father's slender arms and being lifted high into the air.

"Oh, child, not today," his father said.

He didn't lift the boy. He could barely bend over to kiss him on his forehead before walking into the room and carefully sitting on the floor. His body was stiff with pain. The boy walked over to his father.

"Run along," his mother interrupted. "Your father's worked hard today. Run along and play."

The little boy ran outside to the nearest tree. He slumped down beside it and pouted, wondering why his dad was always either working or too tired to play.

* * *

Children don't always know they're poor. Father knew. He was observant. He watched his forty-year-old father carry a workingman's tools and bend like a bow as he dragged himself home at the end of each day. He watched his father toil from dusk until dawn and still struggle to feed his family. He watched my grandfather and noticed he never touched a book. He saw the better-dressed gentlemen in the nearby city of Mehtar-Lam, just ten miles away, carry and talk about books. Father was embarrassed.

Father also saw that the lighter-skinned children were considered more attractive and received more attention. The most beautiful ones had blue and green jewels in place of the more common brown eyes, such as the ones through which Father viewed the world around him. And their hair looked as if an angel had stirred milk into their locks while they were sleeping. Father knew he couldn't change his looks, but he knew he could change one thing to make him special. At the tender age of five, Father made a promise to himself.

"No matter what," the skinny kid who resembled his father said, "I will learn to read and write."

* * *

Saikanda, a small village in the eastern district of Laghman, is just northeast of Kabul. An arch of mountains sits to the north of the village, where it hugs an ancient trade route. Nomadic sheepherders favored the area for the mountains' protection from winter winds. My family favored it for the same reason, especially because it was home and had been our home for generations. The earth around us vibrated with the dust of our ancestors' bones. Their hopes and dreams lived within us.

Winters in Afghanistan—especially in Kabul—are cold, but they are milder in Saikanda. Still, without proper clothing and blankets, even a mild winter can threaten the lives of Saikanda's villagers. Only resourcefulness and planning kept us alive. Throughout the summers, we harvested wild plants, dried them, and stored them to use as food and fuel during the months when nothing grew.

Father's family, the Alikhails, was one of five family groups that lived near the foot of the mountains. His entire extended family lived as a clan inside a *qala* (a huge fortlike complex). Each family lived in its own separate mud-brick shack, surrounded by a courtyard housed within a private wall, which was also built out of mud-bricks. One larger wall encompassed the entire compound of homes.

No matter how high the walls stood around each home, they were no match for the bonds of family and friendship that bound the village together. Nearly all of the villagers in Saikanda knew each other. The local men gathered every morning in the common area around the mosque, where they sat and talked. There, they watched the sun rise from its slumber. Their bare hands and feet soaked up the sun's warmth as their ears drank up the local news and gossip. Then, warmer and satisfied, the men rose and dispersed to their farms for another day of work.

One morning when I was six years old, I got up early so I could join Father for the informal meetings at the mosque.

"Mohammad," Father said when he found me standing by the door, "such gatherings are for grown men."

I felt my face get warm with disappointment.

Father noticed and explained, "Come here." He kneeled down in a rare moment of intimate sharing. "One morning, when I was your exact age and in my first year of school, I woke up early and discovered it was raining hard outside. Since our school didn't meet in a building, I knew class would be canceled. I was relieved not to walk fifteen miles to and from my lessons that morning. Rather than go back to bed, I did just as you did this morning. I waited for my father by the door. After all, rain never stopped the men from working. Unfortunately, upon seeing me, my father made the mistake of letting me join him."

"He must have really loved you," I said.

It was a meager attempt to manipulate a man who was beyond such acts. He heard the words, but he immediately continued his story.

"I felt special and loved as my father and I walked side by side through the rain at dawn. My pride grew when we joined the group of men under a shelter. I saw their delight at my presence. They poured me a small cup of tea, shook my hand, and treated me with respect as they finished up their chatter.

"Then, my father spoke, 'Hey, I just remembered something.'

"I was sure he was about to brag about my schooling. But he asked the men, 'Did I tell you about the time this kid drowned?'

"My eyes grew to the size of the teacup in my hand. I couldn't believe what he had said. I was about to make a gesture to stop him when a man spoke up from the crowd.

"'No, tell us!' he said with excitement.

"The group turned and looked at me with hunger in their eyes. They were hungry for another juicy story to tickle and lift their downtrodden spirits.

"'Well, last summer, he and his younger brother … you all know Shir … went swimming in the river. Out of nowhere, a strong current came and swept this child downstream and under the water. I tell you, he was so scared that he thought he was dead at one point. Didn't you?'

"Your grandfather turned to me as he draped an arm around me and clinched my shoulder, prompting me to respond.

"'Uh ... yeah,' I said to the men. I burned with embarrassment.

"'You know what my younger son did? Oh, heck, go ahead and guess. You'll never guess in a million years!'

"One man from the group obliged and said, 'Don't tell me that young Shir Mohammed jumped in and saved his older brother!' The men laughed. I smoldered inside and tried to step behind my father to take cover from their heckles, but he wouldn't have it. He held me beside him.

"'Ha! Little Shir Mohammad ran home as fast as his three-year-old legs could carry him and said, 'Mommy! Mommy, my brother has drowned! Can I have his milk tonight?'"

"The group of men exploded with laughter. Eventually, my embarrassment turned to rage as nobody inquired about how I ended up saving my own life by pulling myself above the water, crawling out of the river, and walking home until I ran into my mother, who was rushing to find me."

"Father," I said, "Weren't you mad at Uncle? I mean, that he left you?"

"Oh, no," Father said, laughing. "We were so hungry then that I might have done the same thing. I knew then, as I know now, that we love each other. No matter how much you love someone, you've got to eat."

Father continued laughing, but I felt sad.

I asked, "What about Grandfather? Weren't you mad at him?"

"Not for long," Father said. "I remember not knowing why that story was funny, but I felt it helped them somehow make it through the day. So I quickly forgave Father and the others. I just knew that children shouldn't understand that kind of humor. That's why you are too young to join me."

In the evenings, my grandfather and the other hard-working men put away their hoes and ploughs and gathered again at *dukan* (the general shop) to finish out the day with a cup of hot tea and maybe some more "funny" stories.

By the time the sun returned to its slumber, the men weren't the only ones who had exercised their muscles to soreness and depleted their bodies of energy after a long day of work. By sunrise, most women were well into their daily chores. They drew and carried water from the local river, fed the animals, washed and mended clothing, tended to the children, and prepared the meals. By sunset, the women were exhausted, too.

Social roles are ingrained in Afghans. Very early in life, a girl knows she will tend to her parents' home and family until she marries. Then she will take care of her new home and family. A boy knows he will work hard on the farm for his father. One day, he will need to support a family of his own.

Unlike the other children in his village, Father didn't drop out of school after only a year of instruction in order to help out on the farm. He charmed my grandfather into letting him keep going to school until he learned to read and write. My grandfather was proud of his son who walked fifteen miles to and from school every day. He was especially proud that, by the time he was only twelve years of age, his son had become the only literate person in the village of Saikanda.

Shortly after completing the sixth grade, my grandfather died of "old age" in his late forties. Father had no choice but to quit school and work the family's twenty-two-acre farm with Shir Mohammad. At least he had kept his promise to himself to become a literate man. And he would keep another one. He would see that his children were literate as well as educated. There was no way he could have known then that this second promise would one day lead to his own arrest and torture.

* * *

As a young man, Father's abilities to read and write—along with his sister's husband's connections—earned him an entry-level job as a bookkeeper in Mehtar-Lam. It was a low-paying job, but he was a married man with two children by that time.

He enjoyed going to work. A job gave him prestige. Even more importantly, it gave him the opportunity to use his charm. Even on his worst days, Father could have talked an orange into shedding its peel.

Every morning, as his brother headed out to the farm, Father walked ten miles to the government building where he took his place in an office among the other low-level workers. Despite the lack of official distinction, Father's desk was different. It had become a place where top officials stopped by to say hello and ask about his family. At his desk, he exchanged bits of information with his superiors as he slowly wove a network of connections that would become very useful one day. His superiors respected the tall, dark worker from the small village up the road. They admired his work ethic and high regard for education.

Later, with four sons at home, he would meet Miriam on a business trip to a nearby county. He fell in love with her at first sight. Shortly after that meeting, she and her family agreed to a marriage. It's hard to turn down an educated man's potential.

* * *

Throughout all his working life, people admired Father. I was shocked the first time I heard one of his colleagues say that, no matter how busy Father was, he always made time for his friends and co-workers.

"Ha!" I thought. "What a joke!"

This colleague also said he appreciated the on-target advice that streamed from Father's thin lips. It was as natural as a nightingale's song. It surprised me that so many people could adore a man I found so intimidating. But Father was different at home.

"Darling," Mother called out to her husband as she approached respectfully.

Silence.

"Mohammad," Mother said as she drew nearer.

This time, she got right in his line of sight and stood in the middle of the cloud of cigarette smoke that sat in front of him.

"Yes," he said.

"Money," she said. "I need more money to shop for the feast."

"Hmm?" he barely asked.

His tone implied that he was surprised. After all, he had already given her money for the feast.

"Well, yes," Mother completed his thoughts. She was good at that. "You already gave me money. I already went shopping. But you have invited four more families since then. What shall I feed them if I don't go shopping?"

Nodding, Father reached into his pocket and pulled out some rupees for her.

"Thank you," she said. "Oh, it really is kind of you to invite everybody."

"Uh-huh," Father said, returning to his thoughts and cigarette.

A quiet man, he was often seemingly obsessed with thought. He rarely smiled and always smoked. Every day, he turned two to three packs of cigarettes into ash. In fact, he reeked of smoke. I could often smell him approach before I heard him, but that was not unusual for the men of that time. They worked hard. Cigarettes helped them relax.

Father also drank a lot of tea, which he preferred dark and strong. He drank tea, smoked cigarettes, and thought about the future. He demanded silence and order. I often thought of him as a hawk. His entrance into a room was the equivalent of a pause button. Everything stood still. The children stopped running. The women stopped arguing. He would look around and then walk over to his favorite spot. Upon taking his seat, he would light a cigarette. Mother would kneel as she served him a cup of tea. Then Miriam, his second wife, his prize, would sit tall after taking her place by his side.

"Miriam, my dear," Father would say as she moved hesitantly into the room. Her soft, brown eyes were wide. Her gentle face was tilted slightly.

"Good morning," she'd reply.

"Come," he'd say. "Sit by my side."

In the early days of their marriage, her response would be quiet and demure. "Well, actually, I was helping with the wash today."

"No, no," he'd say, taking her hand. "Please, sit by me. I'd much rather have you by my side."

Mother would sometimes walk in. Miriam would blush at the difference between them. But that changed. Miriam eventually expected Father's favor, and she stopped blushing.

Mother said, "Father had very important things to do."

But he would always just sit. I wondered what work of great consequence was achieved by sitting on one's rear end.

Mother said, "He is thinking of ways to improve our life, so we needed to be very quiet."

I wondered how she could stick up for him.

* * *

Despite the fact that Father worked in an office, he still helped his brother on the farm. Together, the brothers worked hard to grow tall fields of wheat, corn, and rice. They saved the money they earned from their crops and added it to Father's income from the government job. After several years, the brothers could afford to make a drastic change for their growing families.

Father decided there was only one way that his sons, who were only babies at the time, would receive a better education. We would need to move to Kabul.

As the capital of Afghanistan, Kabul was considered the land of opportunity. On a leap of faith, Father and his brother left their jobs and moved their families, which included me as well as Miriam's first child, to join the throng of thousands of unemployed Afghans in Kabul who were hoping for better work and a better life. Father was lucky because he had connections from his government job.

Both brothers found jobs at a construction company. They worked as hard as they could and scraped by on as little as possible. They even saved some money. They eventually started their own business and secured construction projects from the government and large commercial businesses. It wasn't too long before they were able to return to Saikanda and open a business of their own.

As their business grew, so did their popularity and respect. As a literate businessman, others often sought out Father for help and advice in dealing with the government. Like many people who had tasted the bitterness of poverty and come to know a sweeter life, he was very generous to friends and family. Just as he had shared his education and knowledge when that was all he had to offer, now he shared his experience, connections, and growing wealth.

One evening, while the men were dispersing from their seats near the mosque, Father hung back with one of his friends. I watched unseen from a nearby tree.

"Tell me, my friend," Father said. "Why are you so down lately?"

"It's nothing, Mohammad," his friend said. "Nothing more than the usual."

But Father didn't believe him. It didn't take much of an astute observer to see that his friend was losing weight. The dark circles under his eyes attested to his lack of sleep.

"And your family?" Father asked. "How are your children?"

His friend didn't answer. He stared off at the horizon. It was one thing to lie about his own well-being. When he didn't know where he was going to get the money to buy the food his children so desperately needed, he sat still and quiet. No lies leaped to his lips so easily. The silence spoke for him.

Father reached into his pocket and pulled out half of his pocket money and offered it to his friend.

"I can't accept that," his friend said.

"We've known each other for years. We went to school together—" Father started.

"For one year," his friend interrupted him, discounting his one year of education before dropping out to tend to his family's farm."

"You are like family," Father said.

"I don't know how I will repay you," his friend said.

"Damned fool!" Father said.

He looked down at the money and considered putting it back in his pocket. He knew his friend wouldn't repay him, but he was still willing to trade his family's feast for a humble meal.

In the end, he didn't return the money to his pocket. He said, "I'm not giving this to you. I'm giving this to your family. I don't expect your children to pay me back."

"Thank you," his friend said, still staring at the horizon.

Father noticed the tears that now streamed down one side of his friend's profile. He seemed pleased with himself.

During those prosperous years, Mother was busy tending to others. It wasn't uncommon for her to find and mend clothing and shoes for Saikanda's poor. At other times, she prepared meals for everyone in our qala and sometimes for the whole village, especially during the Muslim holy days like *Eid-el-Fitr*, the feast at the end of Ramadan, the month of fasting, and *Eid-el-Adha*, the feast of the sacrifice, which honors Abraham's willingness to sacrifice his son for God.

I loved the time of the feasts. Family and friends flowed through our courtyard in groups of around twenty from noon until around five o'clock. We would feed one hundred fifty to two hundred people at each feast. Some arrived with damp clothes, showing they chose to walk through the river that divided our town rather than around it.

Mother and Miriam worked together as hostesses. They filled and refilled dishes of rice, dried fruit, and sweets as long as we had company. Laughter and music filled the air while the best-tasting foods that had ever tickled our tongues filled our bodies.

Before the feasts, my brothers and I boiled and colored eggs for the much-anticipated egg fights. Our family and guests also brought eggs. The object of the game was to hit someone else's egg and break it without breaking yours. The holder of the last intact egg was the winner. As the contestant field narrowed, others would start to bet on who would win. They'd pass the eggs around and tap them on their teeth to help them predict a winner.

As children, we were delighted to receive ten rupees from our father, uncles, and others, who the generous spirit of the feasts inspired. Our dirty hands collected the money throughout the day. We went to sleep at night with dreams of trips to *dukan*, where we planned to trade our treasure for pockets filled with sweets.

"Nasir, stop that!" I yelled at my parents' third son, who was four years older.

I picked up my stride to keep up with him.

"Stop what?" he asked, laughing as we walked home from *dukan*. The other children were far behind us. "Am I going too fast for you? Can't keep up?" He took his right arm and slugged me on the shoulder. "You'll have to work hard if you want to keep up with me." He flexed his twelve-year-old biceps and pounded his chest. "I'm going to be tall and strong like Father."

"What are you talking about?" I asked. "I want you to stop eating your candy, or you won't have any by the time we return."

"So what?" he asked, turning his strut into a run and leaving me behind.

"'So what?'" I thought to myself.

I wanted to savor each sweet treat as I rolled it around in my mouth and across my teeth. This was heaven to me, but I didn't have the insight to know why.

At that time, I didn't know why I wanted those candies to last forever. Years later, I see that the money and the treats had a sentimental value to me. I cherished the tokens of love thrown my way, especially the ones from Father. He was as stingy with his affection to his family as he was generous to others. Those rupees reminded me that, no matter how stern he was, he did love me on some level.

* * *

Outside the family, Father was generous to a fault. His generosity, in combination with his trusting nature and beneficiaries who took advantage of that trust, proved to be his downfall. He lost most of his small fortune through uncollected loans and faulty business plans. He had made money, but he didn't know how to manage it. By the time my brothers and I entered school in Kabul, we were poor again.

But Father still had his education. He saw great value in owning something that nobody could take away from him. He demanded that his boys be educated as well. In fact, we would be more than educated. We would be the best.

"What did you say?" Father asked.

The tone of his voice froze his six-year-old son. I panicked and learned then that no matter how strongly you might wish for time to move backward by just one minute, it wouldn't.

"Don't remember?" he asked.

I swallowed. My heart raced.

"Let me remind you," he said, staring down at me. "You asked me for money so you could run to *dukan* for sweets! Do you think I went to school to become the first literate man in my family so I could send my spoiled son to the store to spoil his teeth? Is that what you think?"

"No," I managed.

"That's right, Mohammad," he said. "I did not. Do you know what I am doing with the money I work for?"

"Sending us to school, Father," I said, relaxing a bit.

I had overheard parts of this lecture before. I knew where it was going. He spent the next ten minutes talking about all his sacrifices and all of my good fortune because of it. In that ten minutes, he had convinced me that I had better perform well, better than he even, or all my life would be a waste.

Chapter Three:
Dying Trees

Despite the fact that we weren't as prosperous as we once had been, Father made sure he could move our entire family back and forth between Kabul and Saikanda. This way, my brothers and I could attend the better schools during the summers. Our entire family still maintained connection to our roots during the winters. The transitions were hard on all of us. We were torn between two lives.

* * *

I was crying. Anwar, my best friend, was crying. My four older brothers and three half-brothers were crying. We were getting ready to board the bus to Kabul, where I would start the fifth grade. I should have felt on top of the world as I approached the end of elementary school, high school is grades seven to twelve in Afghanistan, but I didn't.

Father wasn't crying. He was saying good-bye to Miriam. Mother and my sisters were telling us they'd join us as soon as the weather was warmer and that we, all twenty-one of us, would be together again soon. Anwar and I stood apart from everybody else. We were exchanging one last good-bye.

"You'll be okay, Mohammad," he said. Tears filled his brown eyes and streamed down his cheeks. "But what am I going to do without you?"

"Come on, buddy, you'll be all right," I said, looking at my dear friend through wet eyes.

I wasn't really sure if I believed the words as they came out of my mouth. But I said them anyway. Anwar smiled.

Both of Anwar's parents were gone. One had died of a heart attack. The other died of a liver problem. At only twelve years old, he was the oldest boy in his home, so he was the head of the household. Anwar took care of two younger brothers and one younger sister. His older sister was married and gone.

Anwar's family was very poor. When his parents died, all they had to leave him was a donkey, cow, and mud shack. The walls of his home were so low that we couldn't stand up straight without hitting the roof with the tops of our heads. Anwar was so used to bending down to avoid bumping his head that, even when he wasn't in his own home, he slouched.

The roof of the shack was made of sticks. When it rained, the water collected, soaked the wood, and leaked puddles onto the middle of the floor. No matter where we were or what we were doing, Anwar routinely hunted for sticks to patch up the roof.

* * *

Anwar and I had walked toward the mountains on the day before I left. I'd hardly said a word.

"Come on, Mohammad," he said. "What do you want to do?"

"Nothing, buddy," I said.

"Nothing?" he asked. "That won't cheer you up."

I could tell that he was staring at me, but I didn't look up at him. Instead, I looked down at the ground beneath me and stuffed my cold fists inside my pockets. My entire body was stiff. I clenched my jaw as I thought about leaving the next day.

Anwar stopped walking and reached into his pocket. I stopped beside him and turned to see more clearly what he was doing. He had two pieces of bread in his hand.

"Come on, buddy," I said. "Let's keep going. Hey, what are you doing?"

"You know what," he said. A light twinkled in his brown eyes.

"Keep your bread, Anwar. You'll need that." There was a sharp tone to my words, a reminder that he was poorer than I was. "I just want to get to the mountains one last time and sit."

"Sit and sulk?" he asked. "Come on, Mohammad, let's go have some fun. Let's go see Padawan." He closed his hand over the bread, turned around, and walked away.

"Anwar," I called out to stop him, but he just picked up his pace.

"Anwar!" I yelled.

His quick pace turned into a jog.

"Anwar!" I yelled again.

He kept going, and I started after him. When he heard my feet catching up with him, he ran as quickly as he could, but he was no match for me. Nobody was. In no time, I was ahead of him. We ran for several minutes. Before we knew it, we came upon a herd of cows and donkeys grazing as they soaked up the sun.

In the mornings, as the men of Saikanda made their way to the village's common area for tea, the cows and donkeys that were not needed for work that day followed them. From there, Padawan, a short, bald man in his early thirties, led the nearly two hundred animals that had gathered in the village common area to the foot of the mountains, where there were shrubs for them to eat.

Padawan strolled the hillsides, talking to himself and the animals all day, until it was time to return home. Then he led them back to the village common area. From there, the herd dispersed. Cows and donkeys sauntered and galloped in every direction until they reached their homes. In the evenings, Padawan visited the animals' owners at their homes and collected his pay in bread, which he gathered and carried home to his family.

Anwar and I were among the many children who didn't think twice about walking five miles to exchange a piece of bread for a ride on a donkey. Even though we often rode too quickly and fell off onto our heads, it was one of the highlights of life in Saikanda.

* * *

"Here you are," Padawan said as he handed us two ropes. His voice was soft. I often thought it would be better suited for that of a mouse. His short stature and wispy moustache added to the caricature in my head. He pointed a long finger to two strong donkeys grazing nearby. "Take those two. Whoever rides the darker one might want to take it easy. She's been feisty lately."

"Yeah, okay," we said, already walking toward the donkeys.

"You heard him right?" Anwar asked as I tied my rope around the darker donkey.

"Oh, yeah, I heard him this time. Just like last time. Take it easy," I mocked his mousy voice.

We mounted the dusty animals and kicked our heels into their sides. In an instant, Anwar was ahead of me. My donkey didn't move.

"Woo hoo!" Anwar called, circling around and looking back at us. "What are you waiting for? Scared?"

I glared at my friend who had just challenged me. Then I yelled, "Go, boy! Go!"

I kicked my feet into his sides again. This time, I was stronger. Nothing happened.

"Ha! Maybe he's more afraid of you than you are of him! I don't blame him," Anwar said, roaring with laughter.

"Come on, boy! Go!" I ordered, lifting my feet for another kick. The donkey took off before I had time to kick him again. "Whoa!" I yelled, trying to regain my posture.

The donkey was upset. He took off first to the left and then moved to the right. I tried to slow him down, but he sped up. I gripped his neck with all my might, but I felt my body fall to the side. I took a deep breath and let go, hoping the beast wouldn't run over me. I rolled away from him and sat up. I watched as he took off over the meadow. He was soon out of sight. Anwar came up to me. He was laughing.

"That's one feisty donkey," he said. "Too bad you let him get away. Padawan is going to kill you!"

"Oh no," I said.

I turned around and watched as Padawan marched angrily in my direction.

"I told you to be careful!" he yelled.

"No, you didn't!" I said. "You told me to take it easy. I did. It was the donkey who didn't."

We burst into laughter as Anwar dismounted the donkey.

"See you next time!" I yelled.

Then we ran away.

* * *

"I sure am going to miss you," Anwar said as I placed one foot onto the bottom step of the bus.

I turned to him, smiled, and said, "Look on the bright side. You'll be able to look at Najiba without worrying about my brother."

"Yeah, right," he said. "Nasir would kill me."

We broke into laughter as we thought about how silly it was for my brother, Nasir, the most striking boy in our family, and Najiba, the most beautiful girl in our village, to think that their mutual admiration was a secret.

"Mohammad," Father's soft, but stern, voice broke up our laughter. His tone told me that this hadn't been the first time he had called my name. "Mohammad, get on the bus. It's time to leave."

Anwar stepped aside and nodded. "Go on," he said. "I'll be here when you get back."

"Of course, you will, my friend," I thought.

I boarded the bus to Kabul and watched Anwar wave good-bye as the bus drove away. Halfway into the trip, I wiped away my tears and smiled as I stared out the window. After all, I had something to look forward to in Kabul. I had worked at it ever since my first year of school, thanks to a little deception and some help from my brother.

* * *

The deception became more difficult as I grew up and held more responsibility.

"Mohammad, where are you going?" Father asked as I passed his perch in front of our house.

"To water my tree," I said, holding the water-filled bucket in my hand.

"Good," he said, nodding. Smoke puffed from his mouth and formed a grey cloud.

In Kabul, Mother assigned each of the children a list of chores. One of which was to water "our" trees. We had a lot of fruit trees on our property, including fig, pear, apple, apricot, and cherry. The only way the trees survived the spring and summer was if someone regularly drew water from the well and watered each of the thirsty trees. The chore required multiple trips between the well and the trees. It took quite a bit of time. That year, my duty was to care for a cherry, apricot, and apple tree.

I had better things to do with the opportunity to slip by Father. My trees weren't doing well. I turned around and walked until I was out of Father's eyesight.

"Come here, *Bad-bakht*," Mother said to me a few days later as I returned home from my classes.

"Yes, Mother?" I asked, smiling.

I approached her, careful not to get too close to her nose. She had an excellent sense of smell. My body had just been drenched in a fresh layer of sweat.

"Tell me," she said, peeling a potato for tomorrow's meal. "I was walking around the grounds today to check on our fruit trees." She glanced at me. Her eyes went from my head to my toes and up again. "I noticed that one of them wasn't thriving as well as the others." She placed the skinless spud in a large wooden bowl and picked up another potato to peel. "I noticed it was the cherry tree under your care." Her wrist moved back and forth around the potato. "I decided to take a walk around the entire grounds and saw that none of your trees were doing well."

"Tell me," she said, pausing to pick up another potato. "What are you doing with your time?"

I stared at her, but I didn't know what to say. It felt as if she were asking me two questions at once.

Sighing, she said. "Have Nadir show you how to water the trees properly."

"Okay, Mother, I will," I said.

With only two-and-a-half years between us, Nadir, Mother's fourth son, and I were very close. From that day on, my older brother watered the trees for me ... when he remembered. I continued to sneak out and join the other boys in our neighborhood for soccer, the one thing Kabul could offer that Saikanda could not.

Until that third-grade year, when I was nine, the children in *Debori*, our Kabul neighborhood, played very disorganized games of street soccer. Then Farid stepped in.

Everyone, children and adults alike, admired Farid and his family, especially his brother Ihsan. Farid was a champion of sports; Ihsan was a champion of the soul. I would learn to admire Ihsan later. Right then, our local hero was the brother who had once played soccer for the national team of Afghanistan.

The local legend lived and breathed the game. Itching to become involved in the sport again, he offered to turn the unruly boys of *Debori* into a team. He even offered to organize matches for us. Until then, we had only played against each other. At best, we had only played randomly. We had a general idea of how things worked, but we had never belonged on a true team, and we had never played against a true opponent.

He knocked at the doors of all the boys' homes to explain his intentions and collect ten rupees from each family. Most parents were excited for their children and happily handed over the money. I knew how Father felt about anything that took time away from my studies, so I managed to get the rupees from Mother without tricking her. I took the money to Farid before he got to my house. Our new coach gathered all the money and bought everyone matching uniforms. We practiced where we had played for years, but now we grew under Farid's guidance.

"Okay, guys," Farid said, guiding us around the perimeter of our field and marking the sidelines with a stick.

It was time-consuming. I only wanted to get on the field and kick the ball.

"You've got to pay attention to these lines," said Farid. "One day, maybe I'll mark them with paint or … Hey, what are you guys doing out there?"

"Oh, come on," one eager child named Omar yelled. "Let's play already!"

"Play? You want to play?" asked Farid. "Then run home. If you want to learn skill, then sit there patiently and train your eyes to watch out for these lines!"

This was new. Until this point, we had just run around our poorly defined "fields" without regard to boundaries. Despite our complaints, nobody left. The boys who sat there watching Farid shared a dream. We all wanted to be on the national team.

After a couple weeks of practice, it was time to put on the uniforms. I wore mine under my clothes and left the house without notice. But I still felt a knot in my stomach as I walked out the door and went away from my home. Father had a peculiar way of being present even when he wasn't.

I walked to the team's meeting point and shed my outer layer of clothing. As the other team members showed up, I saw we were all dressed in the same uniform. My knotted nervousness turned into excitement. We matched, and we were on a team.

We walked to the field for our first official game. It wasn't a soccer field. It was just an area that happened to have two utility posts that we could use. The other team showed up. An hour later, I tasted real victory for the first time. I was hooked. From that moment on, soccer was more than a game I played in my free time. It was something I thought about constantly and practiced every chance I got.

* * *

This year, I was a member of our fifth-grade team. I wasn't the best player, but the others liked me because I was extremely fast and known for making a quick score. I liked soccer because it helped me forget about what was going on at home.

Life in the city was hectic. My family argued daily, almost nonstop. Mother and Miriam usually instigated the arguments. The majority of the disputes were based on whose children had more or better food or newer clothes to wear. Years later, I realized their arguments had nothing to do with the children. They were covert ways to release the frustration both of them felt toward Father. After all, what woman likes to think that she alone isn't good enough?

Nonetheless, to us children, we were just normal brothers and sisters. The arguments put us in a very awkward position. We tried not to take sides with a parent and battle each other. Rather, we just tiptoed around and tried to avoid the fights altogether.

These times were hard on everyone, especially my brothers and me. We were in school, and Father demanded excellence, which required a lot of study. We rose early in the morning and walked five miles to school. We endured the usual ridicule from peers. It even came from the teachers. Then we returned home, where it was always as loud as recess until our father walked through the door. His commanding presence did have its benefits.

We didn't have a quiet library in town, where we could have retreated to study. So we made do in our small house, which always shook with laughter, crying, whining, jumping, and running. It was almost impossible to study. I didn't have a desk or special place where I could lay out my books and papers. Instead, I could have easily lost my school supplies to the chaos of our home. I poured all the discipline and control I could into studying. I somehow managed to draw a mental curtain around myself. I was able to block out the noise and action and focus on my homework.

On many nights, I sat in a small corner of our home, studying well past the time that the last baby sobbed himself to sleep. It was late, but it was quiet. My mind could take in the information that streamed before my eyes. I cherished those moments of solitude with the yellow light of a candle lighting the pages of my books. The light eventually would burn out. I would lay my head on the ground. My body would sink from exhaustion into a deep sleep. When I couldn't sleep, I thought about Saikanda and longed to return to the country life I loved so much.

* * *

When Nasir couldn't sleep, he thought about Najiba. In his spare time, he created a dumbbell by connecting two five-gallon buckets with a metal rod. He then filled the buckets with concrete and used the dumbbell for exercise. Over the school year, he sculpted his large frame into a masterpiece that made young girls swoon and men of all ages jealous.

He was perfect. In fact, he was fruitful. Like a tree that never failed to produce the sweetest fruit, he grew admirers and accomplishments. Everyone he met wanted to become his close friend. He did everything with ease. In addition to his excellent looks and physique, he had a wonderful heart. He was very considerate and kind. He made sure that we, his younger siblings, had what we needed. If anyone bothered or intimidated us, his presence alone would protect us. We were in awe of him. We wanted to be just like him when we grew older.

Father admired him, too. Nasir stood six feet tall. With his dark complexion and hair, he resembled our father the most. Nasir was Father's pride and joy. As much time as they spent together, Father had no idea that Nasir's heart and mind belonged to Najiba.

I could tell. I recognized Nasir's parched and withering spirit as I looked closely at him that year. I noticed something was missing. He looked as if he were dying for the water he left behind in Saikanda. Somehow, with everything that was going right, the one thing that was going wrong was really going wrong. Najiba was like a thorn in the bottom of Nasir's foot. He was limping. Soon, his back would ache. Eventually, his neck was in pain. At that time, I had no idea that the extent of damage that one strategically placed thorn could cause. After all, this thorn wasn't really in his foot. It was in his heart. I looked at him and saw one of my dying trees.

Chapter Four:
Trapped Birds

Although winters in Saikanda were considered mild compared to those in Kabul, most of my childhood friends had a hard time during those months when I returned between school years. They didn't own a pair of shoes, and their clothing offered little protection from the cold wind. After years of being handed down, their shirts and pants were ripped and patched into a tattered, wearable quilt. Still, they were proud of what they had, and they worked hard to make the most out of their clothes by keeping them as neat and clean as possible.

Even though our father had lost a lot of money, we children still didn't have to work as hard as our friends did when we returned to Saikanda for our summer breaks. There was plenty of time for me to visit everyone I knew and for Nasir to visit with Najiba.

* * *

"Do you think they'll get married?" Anwar asked me.

"I don't know. I doubt it," I replied.

"Why not?" asked Anwar. "They're perfect for each other. They'd make the most beautiful children ever."

"I think my uncle has someone else in mind for Nasir," I said.

"Who?" Anwar demanded to know. "It doesn't matter. Your uncle doesn't have the final say."

"No," I said. "But Father listens to him. You know how my uncle feels about Najiba's father."

The two men were bitter enemies. Unfortunately, because of their entrenched rivalry, much more than the walls of our homes separated the two lovebirds.

It wasn't until later that I realized how keenly aware of those walls Nasir was.

"What do you care anyway? I thought you wanted to marry Najiba," I said, mockingly.

I closed my eyes and pecked kisses into the air to tease him. But I stopped when I saw Anwar's expression. We both knew that Najiba's father would never give her permission to marry someone as poor as Anwar.

"Let's go to my house for tea," he said, changing the subject. "I have sugar!"

* * *

Many times, I burned with embarrassment as my friends scrambled to find sugar when I arrived for a visit. They didn't have sugar to soften their own cups of tea, but they would send a younger child scurrying over to the next house to borrow some for their guests.

That's the way it is in Afghanistan. No matter how hard life is or how little we have, we put our guests, friend and stranger alike, first. We give them the best of what we have, and we don't expect anything in return.

Six years later, after the fighting started, around ninety members of our extended family and friends from Saikanda would seek refuge with us in Kabul. It took Father years to pay off the light and water bills that the extra people accrued, but he didn't ask anyone for a dime in exchange for his hospitality. More significantly, he didn't hold a grudge.

Nearly twenty years later in South Carolina, I would encounter a much different circumstance that would prompt me to reflect on the nature of my country's generosity. I had built a new life in the United States. I'd paid $23,000 for an out-of-town lawyer to help me recoup the damages I had suffered in a deceitful real estate transaction, which had cost $58,000 to repair termite damage.

When the lawyer visited for the trial, he complained he didn't have anything to do in the evenings. Naturally, I invited him to a weekly soccer match that I helped organize. I even loaned him the equipment he needed to play. Weeks later, I scanned an itemized bill for his work and noticed the lawyer had charged me to play soccer. I didn't sleep that night, but it wasn't because of the bill. I could pay that. I didn't sleep because I thought of how prosperity and poverty had nothing to do with generosity and greed. One would think that, the more one had, the more generous one would be.

* * *

I swallowed my embarrassment and rushed after Anwar to his small shack. I had often felt guilty that Anwar carried so many responsibilities while I had so few. Ironically, my poorest and busiest friend was also the most generous.

"Here," Anwar said, smiling and handing me a steaming mug of honey brown liquid.

I accepted the tea graciously. I knew Anwar had much work to do, but he didn't seem hurried as we drank our tea. Whenever I stopped by to visit him, he never hesitated to take a break from his tasks, even though that meant he would have to work harder once I left. I sometimes talked him into having a little fun with Padawan. Other times, like that day, I helped him work.

My clumsy hands were no match for his finesse with a plow, but he'd let me give him breaks every once in a while. My rows were never quite straight as his. I'd usually just take a shovel and dig at a particularly hard spot. Together, we'd fill the air with the smell of fresh-turned earth and sweat. The dirt filled our nostrils and dried our mouths, but we would still sometimes sing at the top of our lungs. We'd eventually fall down laughing at how out of tune with each other we could be.

When Anwar and I finished his work, we climbed the mountains that graced the edge of our village. They were at their most irresistible just as the sun was setting.

As it had happened so many times, the beauty of our surroundings caught me by surprise. I watched the sun fold into the horizon and paint the sky as she bade farewell for the day. Then the stars slowly appeared. Magic happened as the rotating crown of jewels revealed her glory above me. The stars were so densely packed and bright that I thought I would be able to grab one if I could just reach up far enough. I wished a giant bird would fly just above my head, let me take hold of its tail, and carry me into the sky so I could reach just one of those stars. Then I would take my treasure to town and sell it, so I could throw feasts for everyone in the village, buy shoes for all of my friends, and build a home with higher walls for Anwar. He deserved to stand tall. Although we'd descend the mountains and leave behind that little paradise, I never quite left behind my dreams.

* * *

When I was in sixth grade in Kabul, I managed to save the three hundred rupees I could gather here and there until I had enough to buy something special. Exams were ending. Our family was preparing to return to Saikanda. I couldn't wait to see Anwar and my other friends. I had thought about Anwar a lot and all the work he had to do on his own. I wanted to take something home to him that would bring him great happiness before winter bore in. I walked the streets of Kabul, searching for just the right thing. One day, I peeked through a dirty shop window and found it, a *saira*.

A *saira* is one of the most beautiful birds in Afghanistan. It's small with a grey body; black-and-white wings; a rich cream-colored beak; and a bright, rosy red spot where its beak meets its small head. The best part about the *saira* is that it sings as beautifully as it looks.

"That is a gorgeous bird, isn't it?" the shopkeeper asked me.

"Oh, yes," I said. "I love to hear them sing."

"The trouble with birds is that they never sing as exquisitely as when they are free," he said.

"This one is singing," I pointed out.

"Yes," he said. "But how much more beautiful would his song be if he could sing from the trees."

"I suppose so," I said.

I thought of Anwar and how much he loved birds. Would his generosity be more blessed and his kindness be more intense if he could fly from his tiny home, his mountain of responsibilities? I bought the small bird and its cage. I carried it with me on the bus to Saikanda.

I ran with the bird to Anwar's house, where I found him carrying a load of sticks to his home. He was excited to see me again, but he turned his attention to the bird as soon as he saw it. He laid down his load and reached for the cage. We took the bird with us to a cluster of trees near the mountains, where we placed the cage down on the ground. It started to sing and attracted another *saira*. Quietly, we backed away from the cage and watched as more and more birds swooped in and filled the trees above our heads. We heard their songs all around us.

"I have an idea," Anwar said, pulling some horse hairs from his pocket.

He stood up. The chorus of birds took to the air and flew away. Only our flightless bird remained.

"Anwar," I said, "you scared them away. Stop it. Come back here."

"Trust me," my friend said.

I tiptoed over to him and spent the next half hour following him from tree to tree, where he set out traps on random tree limbs. The horse hairs were tied to limbs in such a way that, as soon as a bird put its weight on one limb, another branch would move and tighten a hair around its legs. With our traps set, we backed away again and watched as bird after bird was caught by its own weight. We ended up with ten more *sairas*, which Anwar sold in the city. He used the money to stock up on food and supplies for the winter.

Winter came. It was a harsh one. I was thankful that school was out and we were in Saikanda rather than walking to our classes in the harsh weather.

Anwar kept the *saira*, along with his cow and donkey, safe and warm inside his home. Most of the villagers in Saikanda opted to share their homes with their farm animals. The donkeys, cows, sheep, and goats were often corralled to one corner of the room, where the animals ate, lived, and eliminated their waste. They made for smelly houseguests, but it was better than the alternative of losing the creatures that helped farm the land and provide food to a frozen death.

The villagers of Saikanda didn't just share their homes with their animals. They shared their drinking water as well. We drew water from a creek that ran off the main river. Most of the animals drank and eliminated their waste into the very same water. Still, people bathed and washed their clothes and baby diapers in the same creek from which they drew the water for drinking and cooking. The people who lived near the end of the creek had the worst water of all. It would become dirtier and darker as it flowed, increasing the risk of cholera, dysentery, and outbreaks of diarrhea.

Despite these conditions, the months we lived in Saikanda passed quickly. No matter how bad our circumstances, we could always find something to do, even without soccer. We had to be creative, of course, but we were good at that. Old rags and nets gave us everything we needed for a volleyball match one day and a game of tackle the next. If we didn't have a ball, we just chased each other around over the hard crust of the earth and the broken glass and metal scraps that littered it. We were numb to the cold and the scrapes and splinters that marked us. In the evenings, I would sneak out of the house to join my friends at *dukan*, where we'd sit in a circle and laugh about what had happened that day.

The mood was always different on my last night in Saikanda. The time to return to Kabul for my sixth-grade year had arrived before I knew it

* * *

"So, it's that time, Mohammad," Omead said, throwing broiled peanut shells into the bonfire. "Time for you to leave us, return to your educated friends, and play your city games, like soccer."

What followed was a series of insults that I had become used to enduring.

"Mohammad's going to go back to the big city and suck up to his teachers so they'll keep letting him back."

"Oh, yeah, he's not as smart as he thinks. They just let him in so all the others can feel smart about themselves."

"Oooh, high school, I bet you feel like a big man now."

I shrugged off the daggers aimed at deflating my ambitions and turned to look at Anwar. He sat quietly that night as he aimlessly poked a stick at the ground. The mocking grew to a loud rumble, and I could tell that Anwar was upset. He stood up and stabbed the stick into the ground.

"Leave him alone, okay?" said Anwar. "Mohammad's going to make something of himself one day. That's more than we'll ever do. So just shut up."

He turned around and walked off. I jumped up and went after him.

"Thanks," I said to Anwar as I caught up to him.

"It was nothing," he said. He stopped walking long enough to bend over and pick up a rock.

"Do you really believe that?" I asked.

"What?" he asked.

"That I'll make something of myself?" I said. "That I'll be somebody."

"Yeah, I believe it," he said. "I believe you'll get a great job that takes you far from here and you'll marry a wonderful woman because of it. You'll have a lot of sons, and you'll be too busy working to remember the friends you left behind." He threw the rock at the ground. "Damn school. Who in the hell invented it anyway?"

He was right about everything, except for two predictions. I don't have any sons. And I do remember those I left behind. Maybe my life in Kabul gave me the education I needed to get to where I am today. But my life in Saikanda gave me the heart to get here.

Chapter Five:
Faded and Unraveled

Upon our return to Kabul for my sixth-grade year, just like every year before this one, Father led my brothers, my cousins, and me on our annual hunt for school supplies and clothing. This was a very frustrating time for Father, and it was an embarrassing time for us. My family was just one of many who rummaged through piles of secondhand materials and clothing.

"Hey, take your hands off my shirt!" Abdul Mateen yelled.

I looked in his direction. Both he and another kid were holding on to the same pair of Levi's jeans. I scanned the jeans. They looked like they were in excellent condition. Nadir and Nasir briefly stopped their searches and stepped up behind Abdul Muqeem, the second-oldest son, and Abdul Mateen's shoulders. They crossed their arms and stared at the young man. He took one look at Nasir and let go.

"They're not my size anyway," he said before he drove his hands into the next pile of clothes.

The first fight was over. The next would be paying for them.

"One hundred fifty rupees?" Father asked. "That's too much."

"They're in excellent condition," the owner argued. "One hundred rupees," he said again, putting the jeans in Father's hands.

"I don't want them," Father said as he put them back in the other man's hands.

"You don't want them?" asked the owner. "They aren't good enough for you? Here!" He shoved them into Father's chest. "Take them for free. Have them!"

"I don't want them," Father said.

"They're yours!" said the owner.

"Eighty rupees," Father said calmly. "I will pay eighty rupees."

"Fine!" the owner said.

We had to be quick and on the ball to score the real deals like Adidas shirts and Levi's jeans, but we usually ended up with outfits that never quite matched or fit properly. Western countries donated most of the secondhand clothing that we wore. The local bazaar was filled with items that came from all over Europe, Australia, and the United States. Shoppers could find just about anything they wanted among the faded fashions and worn wares. The price would be much less than they would have cost new. We shopped for everything we needed at the bazaar. We even bought used school supplies there.

* * *

Though the public schools were free and the government tried its best to provide most of the materials to students, basic supplies like notebooks and pens were so expensive that their cost alone was a roadblock that kept many Kabul families from sending their children to school.

The schools themselves were of second-rate quality, making it hard for those who could afford to go to school to want to stay there. The tables rocked and were propped up for stability. The chairs were weakened from years of use. The books were either outdated or had pages missing. Usually, it was both.

The school regimen was very strict. The teachers were allowed to beat us for simple infractions of the rules, like speaking too softly or too loudly when called upon.

"Excuse me, sir," I said to Zia, the third-grade teacher who had just handed me three books, two of which were missing pages, for the school year.

"What do you want?" he yelled at me, obviously mad I had interrupted his process with the next student in line.

"These two books," I said, gulping, "are missing pages. Can I have new …?"

"What?" he yelled.

The metal feet of his chair screeched across the dusty floor as he stood up. He stomped toward me, took the books out of my hand, and started to hit me with them. I threw up my arms to protect me, and he kicked me in the legs. I fell to the floor. He kicked me again, and I slid five feet away. He picked up the discipline stick he carried and started to beat me all over my body.

"Who do you think you are that you should get special books?" he asked. "Good books? Huh?"

"Nobody," I said. "I'm sorry."

I never asked for a better book again. I did, however, learn to take extremely accurate notes in class.

On top of the normal stresses of school, hunger also stood in our way. After walking miles to school without breakfast, many students could not concentrate and memorize. The clock ticks slower when one's stomach is empty and rattling with yesterday's crumbs. I remember wondering if classes were ever going to end and if I'd have the energy to walk through the doors and get back home. The luckiest students were those who had a cup of tea with some sugar and wheat bread. For the most part, students either went to school hungry or with a small piece of cornbread and tea without sugar. Although I was usually hungry, I was fortunate because I lived closer to school. There were days, however, that I gladly would have traded this proximity for a slice of prosperity or at least clothes that fit properly.

At times, those clothes were the reason I hated school. On many days, I cried because the holes in my shoes and pants embarrassed me. The holes were very small, but I then thought they screamed, "Hey, look at me! I'm poor!" Sure, a lot of us were poor, but even the poor have a hierarchy that a need to feel better than somebody else fueled. It sometimes hurt so badly to be picked on. I wished I could just fade away and run out of the classroom. I wanted to go home and never return. I wanted to be anywhere other than there. But my family, especially Father, was determined I would stay in school, appreciate it, and do well.

Father inspired the best in us, but it wasn't through empathy and understanding. Rather, it was through a force similar to that applied at school. The only difference was that his hurt worse. He was Father. I excelled at school.

* * *

This, however, was the start of a brand-new school year for me. The sixth grade was the start of the last year of my elementary education. Finally, I was at the top. If all went well, I'd get into Habibia High School and attend grades seven to twelve at the same school where my four older brothers had been accepted.

The United States funded Habibia High School, one of the most popular high schools in Afghanistan. It was in better condition than any other school I had ever seen. The books were up-to-date, and they had all of their pages.

As one of the best-looking and strongest guys in the school, Nasir was one of the most popular boys. Mere acquaintance with Nasir and his friends, Najib, Fauad, and Farid, who was a different Farid from the one who organized our soccer games, was instant protection. As Nasir's brother, I was going to be invincible.

The usual stream of Nasir's friends started to flow in and out of our home as soon as we returned to Kabul.

"Nasir, how are you, my friend?" asked Najib, shaking his hand and stepping forward to embrace his best friend.

Nasir hugged him, but his demeanor was distant. It was awkward.

"I am well," my brother said. "How have you been?"

The words were there, but the flavor, that is, the inflections and his posture, were not.

"Great, yeah," he said. "I'm great."

"Hey, Mohammad, ready for another year?" he asked as he turned my way.

He lowered his brow and flashed his eyes to the left toward Nasir. That was his way of telling me that something was off.

"I bet you can't wait to play soccer again," he continued.

"Yeah," I said, nodding, which was intended to answer his look, not his question. "I can't wait."

"Well, Nasir," Najib said, focusing his attention again on my brother. "We've got a lot of talking to do. Shall we go meet the others?"

"Of course," my brother answered.

He and his friend said good-bye to me and turned to leave. I watched them walk away. Seeing the two show horses side by side, I could really tell that something in my brother was different. Nasir was shrinking. His friends continued to stop by and invite him out, but he joined them increasingly less as the year went on.

Nasir put on a good face around town. But, by the time he got home, he didn't have the energy to keep up the charade that he was in good spirits. In reality, his spirit was broken. He knew our father would listen to our uncle. Promising Nasir to our uncle's wife's relative would be a favor Father would want to give.

"Nasir," our oldest brother, Abdul Mateen, would say, "You've got to get that girl out of your head!"

At first, Nasir argued, "But she's the only one for me! If I can't be with her, I don't want to be with anybody!"

Then Nasir became poetic. To Abdul Mateen, he said, "She is a sun that will never set." To himself, he said, "She is a rose that will never fade."

Soon after he started talking to himself, he stopped making sense.

"A wall. That's all. I dance there. I sing there. I will die there. No, I got it. I will tear it down. And grow another," he said, laughing as he scanned the room. His beady eyes darted from side to side.

Then Nasir, the guy who used to walk into the middle of a room and draw all eyes to him, crept around the house with his back close to the walls. He felt safe there because there was less to scan. He withdrew. He stopped going out with his friends and stopped going outdoors altogether. His friends stopped coming by and inviting him out. We could no longer brush off his behavior as temporary. Something was very wrong. Maybe it was permanently wrong.

Abdul Mateen decided to get in touch with our father, who, along with our uncle, had decided to stay in Saikanda that year until it was time for the women to join us in Kabul.

"How long has he been like this?" Father asked before going in to see Nasir.

"Two weeks," Abdul Mateen told him.

Father was furious to find out that we had waited so long to get in touch with him. Soon, however, he would understand our denial.

Father recoiled at the sight of his broken son. Nasir was dirty and unkempt. He hadn't shaved or taken a bath, which our family normally took every one to two weeks, for a month.

Upon seeing his father, Nasir jumped to his feet with the excitement of a two-year-old. Only for a brief moment, Father forced a thin smile upon his face. He replaced that smile with a desolate look as soon as his son's face was buried in his shoulder. They embraced for a long time. Father got a taste of Nasir's madness his first night back.

"Nasir, you need to get to bed," Father said to him again.

It felt like it was three o'clock in the morning. I wasn't sure, but I was awake, pretending to sleep.

"Ha ha ha!" Nasir laughed maniacally. I heard him run across the room and bump into something. "Ah!" he screamed.

"Stop that," Father said. "Stop playing with your feet. They're filthy. Don't put your hands in your mouth. Here, let's wash them."

"Don't touch me!" Nasir said.

Nights of manic rampages were followed by days of not eating a complete meal. His presence had waned. He usually just sat in a corner with his arms around his knees. His waiflike frame was barely a shadow of his trademark physique.

In shock, Father needed support. He sent word to the rest of the family in Saikanda that it was time to join him in Kabul.

* * *

Mother wept upon seeing her son. For the first time in her life, she knew that her well-known gift for nurturing would fail her, but that didn't stop her from trying her best to bring her son back to life. The task, which required feeding and cleaning him, helping him go to the bathroom, and constantly watching him, was too big for her. It wasn't long before my uncle took over Nasir's care.

My uncle took him from doctor to doctor.

All of them said, "There's nothing we can do for him."

After months of hope that this was a physical problem that a change in diet or a simple pill could cure, Father realized it was time to take Nasir to a psychiatrist. He wasn't prepared for what he was about to hear.

"I'm not sure what's going on. I need to watch him. I can't help him. You should put him in an institution," the psychiatrist said.

"I'm sorry," Father replied. "I just can't do that to him. He's my finest son."

"Soon, the burden will become too hard for your family to bear," said the psychiatrist. "Trust me, the time will come, and you will have to put him in an institution."

"No," he said. "I can't. My son will never be a burden!"

Father left the psychiatrist's office. A single light of hope flickered in his mind. The thought of locking up Nasir as if he were a wild animal forced Father to turn to nontraditional sources of healing.

"It has to work," he said to himself as he plotted out a plan.

In general, Afghans are very suspicious of modern medicine. Many prefer superstition and spiritual tradition, which Father usually brushed aside as nonsense and the imaginations of the uneducated. All of a sudden, however, nonsense became nectar to his parched heart, and Father was a believer.

One belief common to Afghans is that a visit to the gravesites of certain holy and legendary figures will cure just about any ailment.

"Imagine," Father thought, "what many visits would do for my dear son!"

From that day on, whenever Father had a chance, he whisked Nasir away for a trip to the resting place of deceased deities and do-gooders, where he pleaded and bartered with God to restore his son. Rather than improving, however, the situation worsened for all of us.

Nasir started sobbing during all hours of the night. When I watched him cry, I couldn't help but wonder if a piece of him was left inside, a piece that was mourning the proud man he used to be. At other times, I thought that maybe he was crying because he was alone and lost. He was like a child who had wandered into a dark wilderness, but his wilderness was his own unraveled mind. In a way, I hoped he was not aware of his previous life. I figured it would be easier on him that way. For whatever reason, the crying started and didn't subside.

Our entire family was so upset for Nasir that many of us cried with him while the others tried in vain to sleep. On the rare nights he didn't cry, he was restless. He'd wake up and listen to music or talk to himself. Unable to sit still, he'd move around from room to room throughout the night. To this day, I remember well the sound of his feet as they shuffled across the floor.

While life as we knew it continued to fade inside our home, life outside of our home continued as usual. We went to school, completed chores, kept up with social responsibilities, and put on a face that said that everything was going well. It wasn't long before our entire family was so exhausted, nervous, and sick with worry over what might happen next that Father had no choice but to put Nasir in a mental institution. That breaking point came when no one in our home slept for six nights in a row.

* * *

"I can't take it anymore," my half-brother Obaidullah said. "Tell him to shut up!"

He pressed his hands over his ears in an effort to drown out the moans and cries that haunted him from the next room. He was shaken. We all were.

"Come here, little buddy," I said, putting my arm around him. I did my best to conceal my frustration and console my younger brother. "It'll be okay."

"No, it won't!" he said. "It'll never be okay!"

"It will. Trust me." I spoke the words slowly.

I stared into his eyes. He had my stepmother's big brown eyes, the ones that captivated Father. Right now, they were filled with tears. He nodded and calmed down. I was relieved that I wouldn't have to go into why I knew the screams and wakefulness would soon end.

Two hours later, Obaidullah watched in horror as my older brothers and I helped my uncle and father wrestle Nasir to the ground. Seven men struggled to bind his arms and legs with rope and carry him to a taxi. I watched Father lower Nasir's head into the vehicle and then step in himself.

Later that night, Father returned by himself. I overheard him tell my uncle how he took Nasir to the *darolmajaneen* (house of crazies) at Ali Abad Hospital, where the overseer of the mentally ill chained Nasir to a large post in the middle of a huge room. Finally, our home was silent again, but, ironically, nobody slept.

* * *

The next morning, I skipped school and walked to the hospital. The further I went along the ten-mile trip, the more infuriated I grew. The night before, it had seemed so right, but it now seemed horribly and plainly wrong. I cursed Najiba for being so wonderful. I cursed Nasir for being so weak. I cursed my uncle for not allowing them to marry. Then I cursed Father for not standing up to my uncle and sending my brother to the hospital. My anger grew with every step I took.

Finally, I arrived at my destination. After surveying the hospital from the outside, I knew I'd be able to find my brother behind the window with bars.

"That's where I'd put the crazy people," I thought to myself.

I peeked in and looked around the room before me. I swallowed my gasp. It sank like a brick in my stomach. The people behind the bars wandered and stared as mindlessly as the cows and donkeys that Padawan led through Saikanda, except the mentally ill wandered around a large room under Hashim's watch. Hashim, a tall, mustachioed man with long, dark hair, had been a patient ten years ago. He'd recovered, so the story goes, but, because he didn't have any family to whom he could return, the hospital had armed him with a baseball bat and put him to work. His job was to make sure that everybody did what they were supposed to do and nobody escaped.

Careful to stay out of Hashim's line of sight, I scanned the room for my brother. My anxiety grew by the second as I searched and didn't find him. I searched the zombie faces for a half hour. Still, they wandered around and around without interruption, incident, or inclination.

The zombies showed no sign of awareness until a man opened a set of doors on the far side of the room. Two workers carried in a body, holding him at his wrists and ankles. The zombies paused, looked around for a moment, and then started wandering again, around and around. The workers showed little regard for the human being they carried. They let the body swing from side to side. They dropped it like a dead fish. It lay on the floor next to a set of heavy chains. Finally, they turned around and left the room.

I looked closely and wondered if that person was still alive. I stared at the chest and saw signs of breathing. My eyes focused on the foam spilling from his mouth. I recognized that mouth and realized the body belonged to my brother.

My head spun at the sight of him. All of a sudden, I felt as if I were going to throw up. I sat down with the brick in my stomach and waited. The sun's heat tried its best to send me home as my nausea and dizziness increased, but I didn't back down. I continued to sit there and watch my brother as his chest rose and fell ... rose and fell ... rose and fell.

He woke up two hours later. I waved. My body was stiff from sitting so long. He didn't notice me, so I waved again and with more zeal. My brother spotted me and broke into tears.

"Nasir!" I cried, unable to restrain myself or my tears. "Nasir!"

He got up and stumbled his way through the zombies, moving toward the window that separated us.

"Mohammad," he said between sobs, "you've got to get me out of here. They're going to kill me. They shocked me. They're going to kill me. I'll die!"

I tried to comfort him between his warnings of impending doom. I said things I didn't believe.

"It'll be okay."

"They're not going to kill you."

"You're going to get better."

But he didn't calm down. I looked over his shoulder and saw that Hashim was approaching us. He clenched the bat in his right hand and slapped it into the open palm of his left hand. He walked slowly, but his grimace told me to hurry up and make Nasir move away from the window. I looked at my brother once more. Through a stream of tears, I promised I'd do whatever I could to bring him home.

"Go, Nasir. Now!" I said.

I looked up and locked eyes with Hashim. We stared at each other as Nasir backed away and faded into the crowd of zombies.

* * *

When I returned to the house, I found Mother kneeling on her jainaz (a small prayer rug). She turned to me. From the look on my face, she knew where I had been and how it had gone. I threw my arms around her, and we cried together. This was one of the few times that the warm bouquet of spices that wafted from her skin didn't comfort me.

"If we don't get him out of there," I finally said through my sobs, "he's going to die."

We continued crying together for a couple more minutes. Then we separated from each other and agreed to implore the family for their help in bringing Nasir home.

The idea didn't fly well. Father met our supplications with a firm and frigid no. As the weeks passed, we spoke less of Nasir.

Part of me wanted to return to the *darolmajaneen*. Instead, I also pushed thoughts of my brother aside and sought more to forget about both life at home and the hospital.

* * *

"Where are you going?" Father asked as I was leaving the house.

"To study with Yahya and the gang," I said, flashing a notebook. "We need to work on a project."

He nodded, accepting the excuse that I'd be studying with my best friends in Kabul, Yahya, Shafi, Akbar, and Sameem.

I walked until I was out of sight and then quickened my pace because I was late. I met Nadir around the corner, where I traded him his notebook for my uniform.

"Good luck," he said.

"Hey, buddy, aren't you coming?" I asked.

"Sorry, man, I've got to study for my exam. Next time," he promised.

We parted ways, and I jogged to the soccer field. As the captain of the sixth-grade team, I didn't want to be the last one to make it to the game. I showed up just in time to give a pep talk and lead everyone onto the field.

I watched the other team approach the half line. From their perspective, I was just another player on the field. Inside, however, I was transforming. If Nasir could change, so could I. Only mine was an entirely different transformation.

The other players didn't realize that, at that moment, a part of my central nervous system was unhooking itself from my cognitive brain and tapping into my instinctual reserve. My ears filtered out all sound except those that located and distinguished friend from foe. My mind shut steel doors on all thoughts, allowing information to jump from the point of intake to the point of action without hesitation. My heart laid down its burdens to turn with desire to its true love, winning.

My abilities to follow instinct and make a quick score paid off. With a final run down the field, I knocked in the tie-breaking point we needed to head to the semifinal games. Every cell in my being roared, raising me three feet into the air. My teammates came and lifted me to their shoulders. Slowly, the sound returned to my ears, thoughts seeped into my mind, and my heart once again picked up its burdens. I took off my uniform and returned home.

"Where's your notebook?" Father asked.

"Uh, I must have left it at Yahya's," I said. "He'll probably bring it to me tomorrow at school."

"I see," he said. "How are you doing this year?"

I wanted to give him a lecture on daring to inquire into my studies after everything I'd been through, but I checked myself and decided it was better to give the standard response.

"Great."

It wasn't a complete lie. I was doing very well, considering that between life at home and life on the team, I rarely had time to study. Fortunately, I had developed an ability to memorize the things I heard and read very quickly. Due to last-minute reviews with friends, I was able to remain one of the top students in my class.

I was starting to develop a reputation as a good soccer player and enjoying the admiration that comes with athletic ability. Despite my short height and small frame as well as the rumors about Nasir, I was a giant among my classmates.

The rumors didn't bother me much.

"At least others remembered him," I thought to myself.

At home, it was as if we had forgotten him. But that didn't last for long.

* * *

"Mohammad, get that," Mother instructed.

I walked to the door and opened it. There, before me, stood a withered man with a clean-shaven head and face. He wore hospital clothing. Without hesitation, I embraced him.

"Nasir," I cried. "Good to see you. Come in."

I stepped out of his way so he could enter our home. After a stream of welcomes and hugs from our family, it finally dawned on us to ask Nasir why he had been released.

"Released? Well ... uh ... I wasn't exactly released," he admitted.

We listened as he told us very nonchalantly, "I was lying awake bored last night. I wanted someone to talk to. As I looked around the room, I noticed everybody was asleep. Well, that never happens. Someone's always awake in that crazy place. I thought this might be the only chance I'd have to get out of there. I looked over at the window and wondered if I could bend the bars enough to slip through. I broke the chain to the wall and walked over to the window. Well, the bars bent, and here I am."

Silence.

"That's my boy," Father said. "He placed a hand on Nasir's upper arm and squeezed his muscle. "You always were the strongest one of us. Welcome home."

I wondered, as I'm sure others did as well, if everything was going to be okay now that he was out of the hospital. I worried life would return to the way it was right before he left, but, the more he told us about the hospital, the happier I was that he was out of there.

"You're covered in cuts," Mother said.

"And bruises," Abdul Mateen added as he stared at him in disbelief.

"What happened to you?" Mother asked.

"Nothing, Mother. I'm fine," he said. "The beatings weren't so bad, you know? I feel stronger."

He smiled and looked at our father, but Father looked at him quizzically.

"Why do you keep scratching your head?" Father asked.

"It's no big deal," Nasir said, blushing. "Everyone has it."

"Lice?" Mother asked. "What kind of place is that *darolmajaneen*? If it wasn't so bad, then why did you leave?"

Nasir fell onto his mother's shoulders and whimpered, "It was awful. They beat us. Hashim beat us daily. The doctors shocked us almost as often. I had to get out of there."

After only a couple of days at home, I could tell that something—perhaps the electroshock therapy, medications, or experience of being locked up—had calmed down Nasir. His mind was more organized. It was a little easier to be around him, especially once he started taking his medications. He had been diagnosed with bipolar disorder. After a month of living at home, his friends started to visit again. He soon ventured into town. The spells of madness would come and go after that, but they were more manageable.

Although he would never fully recover his physique, charm, and personality, it looked as if life would almost go back to normal for Nasir. To be on the safe side, however, we decided not to return to Saikanda that winter and the next. After all, our family had a reputation to protect.

* * *

Nasir would leave Afghanistan soon after that year. (At the time I started to write this book, he was living as a refugee in Peshawar, Pakistan.) Before leaving the country, he would finish the twelfth grade and marry our uncle's sister-in-law, to whom our uncle had promised him. He and his wife would hate each other and argue often.

A year after their marriage, Susan was born. Susan, a beautiful little girl, had the saddest eyes I have ever seen. If the anger between Nasir and his wife affected their second child, Quais, his bright smile masked his concern well. He was a very handsome boy with a vibrant personality.

Unfortunately, Nasir's disdain for his wife spilled over to include his children. He paid very little attention to them. In fact, he ignored many of their needs. For example, he neglected to get them vaccinated for polio. Quais came down with the disease and limped for the rest of his life. For most of his adult life, due to his mental disability, Nasir was unable to attain and hold down a job. Consequently, his family was extremely poor. His children, illiterate and uneducated, had a very slight chance of ever changing their fortunes.

* * *

Hardships come with growing up poor in Afghanistan. Although we worked hard to survive, I learned that year in sixth grade that hard work alone wasn't enough. Luck plays a role. Even I, *Bad-bakht*, had my share of good luck. How else could I explain that my brother, who was just as smart as I am and more popular and charming than me, suffered such a setback?

My guilt was enormous, but I carried it. I also carried the fear that I was next. I feared everything I had was about to slip through my fingers. My experiences that year instilled a stubborn drive into my being. It was a drive to live each day and each moment to the fullest.

I had known there were no guarantees in life, but, after that year, I knew that even life wasn't a guarantee of living.

Chapter Six:
Pulse Rate

No matter what was happening at home or at school, soccer could always help me forget about my hardships. One day, it would help ease my pain from the death, destruction, crooks, and corruption that would grip Afghanistan. For my friends and me, it was the drug with which we abused our bodies and numbed our minds. For my land, soccer was the force that could capture a divided nation's attention and hold everyone's breath in the palm of its hand.

Only kite-flying rivals soccer as the most popular sport in Afghanistan. We didn't fly kites merely to enjoy a breezy day. Rather, we flew kites in a fierce battle to see who controlled the last kite in the sky.

One of the most enjoyable things I've ever done is fly a kite. Despite that, I rarely flew kites. The big kite-flying season was at the beginning of winter, which is when we were packing to leave for Saikanda. People in my village just didn't fly kites. Additionally, I didn't have enough money to buy the kites with their special glass-encrusted thread.

Instead, I joined the crowd of observers who walked around the city, watching the kites battle in the air to their death. The homes and fences that enclosed them were close together in Kabul. I ran along the fences and jumped from one to the other as the other children and I followed the kites. Hopefully, if it was my lucky day, I could catch one of the fallen wind soldiers. But I usually returned home with empty hands. Soccer, on the other hand, was free, readily available, and played all year long. Even without a ball, cleats, or nets, soccer always was my game of choice.

In Afghanistan, soccer is as natural to boyhood as make-believe and tag. A young boy grows up rooting for his brothers and cousins against their opponents. He watches their feet carry the ball, which usually wasn't a ball at all, up and down streets. He watches their heads turn from side to side to keep in touch with their teammates. That's how my learning began.

I started playing with the younger children as we fumbled and dribbled with our short legs and small feet until we were big enough one day to join the older players in games. From there on, we played as often and as hard as we could.

As a young boy, before Farid organized us into team *Debori*, I would rush home from grammar school to fit in a game or two before sunset. I met the other boys in our neighborhood streets, where we divided into two teams of testosterone. Day after day, we threw our bodies and souls into a match of skill for control over an onion. We sometimes fought over a potato or even a rock. We propelled any suitable prey between our bare feet as we raced in pursuit of that evening's claim to victory.

The city of Kabul had one main and four smaller soccer stadiums. All of which were reserved for large tournaments only. Without a recreation center or even a park or free space in our neighborhood, we played in the streets, which added a violent opponent, traffic, to the game. We didn't just dodge opponents. We dodged cars. Almost every family I knew had their own tragic story of loss to tell.

My family's tragedy was the death of Wahid, Nadir's brother-in-law. He was only fourteen years old at the time.

"The car hit him and killed him right there on the street. Right in front of his friends," Mother said. She shook her head, burying her tear-stained face in her hands. "He never even saw the car coming."

We were all familiar with fatal soccer stories, but, as children and teenagers do, we categorized them as "events that happen to others." The closest I came to a soccer-related death was in the fourth grade, and it had nothing to do with cars.

* * *

It was a hot summer day. Father held a sickle in one hand and a handful of twisted and braided grapevines in the other. He swung his arm up and down, again and again, as he whacked the sickle against the vines that grew above the entrance to our home. I was unaware that he had received my first set of grades for the year. Else, I certainly would have chosen another time to enter the house.

"Hello, Father," I said as I approached the door.

"Mohammad, come here, please," he said to me.

"Huh?" I asked.

Though soft, the tone of his words shook me from behind. I turned around to face him. His left hand grabbed a fistful of shirt at my chest as he raised his right hand, still grasping the handle of the sharp blade. He brought the blade near my neck. His eyes poured their dark glare into mine.

"If you don't rise from fourth in your class by your next set of marks, I'll cut your throat. Do you hear me?" he said.

Swallowing, I said, "Yes, Father."

He let go of my shirt, shoved me toward the door, and said, "I don't know why I bother with you."

He might as well have been talking about the weather. His words were void of anger. They were spoken as mere factual observation.

"You'll never get anywhere in life because you waste all your time playing soccer," he said, looking at me. His eyes filled with disgust as he noted my dirty appearance. "Go clean up."

"Yes, Father," I said. It was all I could manage to say.

That year, I rose from fourth to second in my class, but Father still wasn't satisfied with me. No matter how well I did at school, he never approved of my extracurricular activity. My commitment to soccer only made him more disgruntled as the months passed. That's when I started to hide it from him.

In general, it wasn't too hard to sneak past him. A part of his mind was always busy thinking about other things, including his work, finances, or his friends and their problems. There were days, however, when he'd be at home sitting on the porch as I, unaware of the bruising on my legs, approached. He wasn't too busy to notice then.

"It's a waste of time," Father said after I returned home from playing soccer one day. "You haven't even completed your schoolwork."

"I'm on my way to do it right now," I said.

"Listen to me, Mohammad," he directed. "You have to put education first. Only fools put games before school. Do you hear me?"

"Yes, Father," I said.

I started to explain that I could do both well, but his words stopped mine.

"Soccer," he said before he paused to take in a deep breath of smoke, "will get you nowhere. It'll distract you. You'll never become anybody. You'll bring nothing but shame to me."

With a flip of his wrist, he released the dark ashes from the end of his cigarette into the breeze. He probed my eyes with his. I wondered if he could read my thoughts. Adrenaline snapped its whip and pulled a noose around my neck. My pulse quickened. I wondered if my own body would deceive me as I decided to play the game in complete secrecy.

* * *

A man's pulse is revealing. Its rate, rhythm, and strength hint at things of which his mind is unaware, doesn't want to admit, or wants to hide. A trained physician uses the pulse to help detect abnormalities in his patients' heart valves and arteries and locate blockages in their bodies. Some Tibetan doctors rely on pulse alone. After listening to it for a few minutes, they are able to offer the patient a complete diagnosis and treatment plan.

A society's pulse, that is, its pace, culture, and economy, indicates its quality of state. In July 1973, the year I started eighth grade, a sudden change in control shocked our nation. Its pulse increased in fear, uncertainty, and excitement.

When Mohammad Daud Khan overthrew his cousin, Mohammad Zahir Shah, not only did he bring an end to forty years of rule under one king, he ended the monarchy altogether and introduced a new era of leadership. It was a democratic era.

The first president in our country's history promised to implement programs that would reward those who worked hard at their jobs. He gained the support of the laymen. He talked about building allegiances with pro-Western countries, much like Pakistan was doing, which endeared him to the educated.

But his verbal commitment to national sports, especially to the creation of a strong national soccer team, boosted morale across the board. His plans infused a new sense of hope into the people of Afghanistan. For the first time in years, the nation buzzed about the growing economy and security to come.

Some remained openly skeptical. Doaud's early efforts to quiet the various factions of the Marxist People's Democratic Party of Afghanistan (PDPA) only united the party's two main groups: the *Khalq* (masses) led by Nur Muhammed Taraki and Hafizulah Amin and the *Parcham* (banner) led by Babrak Karmal.

With Daud focused on forming alliances with pro-Western countries and a small, but focused, Communist movement uniting to oppose him, my country had attracted the attention of a power to the north. Little did we know that another nation had directed its cool gaze upon us and had lifted its iron fingers to take our pulse. It listened, watched, and waited.

* * *

The political climate may have been in flux, but life at Habibia remained the same. At least I didn't start my second year at the high school with the expectation that my peers would take their studies as seriously as I did and Habibia would be an educational utopia. A lot of my classmates had dropped out the previous year. On some days, I wanted to join their numbers, but I decided it was better to be tired and miserable at school and have a place to call home than to drop out and be forced to spend the rest of my life hoping I wouldn't run into my own father.

Despite being smart and wealthy, too many of the students at Habibia felt that life still was worth little. Among my seventh-grade classmates who made it through to the next year were those who skipped school to watch movies downtown. Others sought shelter in shadows as they injected their arms with heroin. No matter how tempted I was to try other forms of escape, I steered clear if it jeopardized my abilities on the field. It was especially important now I had a new goal of playing for the national team.

The regime change had come at a good time for me. In the eighth grade, I started to take soccer more seriously. Daud's devotion to a national team let me believe that my big dreams might become my reality. That year, soccer became my study.

My skills were raw. Lacking formal training, aside the little that Farid offered our neighborhood team when I was younger, I paid attention to the better soccer players who I knew, like my cousin Naim Nassery and others on a team called *Bamica*. Naim helped form the team, which, after only a few years, had already earned a reputation for supplying players to the national soccer team of Afghanistan.

I watched Naim as he pumped his legs, like the pegs of a pinball machine, back and forth. He weaved a web through and around a shuffling wall of opponents, all the while keeping the ball safely between his magnetic feet. I watched the others as individuals and as a team. My mind seized control of the ball as I watched and maneuvered it with the team. My heart already belonged to *Bamica*. Right along with the players, I shouted in victory and agonized in defeat.

"Hey, Mohammad," Naim called to me as I stood on the sidelines during a *Bamica* practice.

"Hey, buddy," I said.

"Come on," he said. "Show us what you got."

My heart raced. I wondered if he meant what I thought he meant.

"Hey, now," he yelled again. "We don't got all day. Get your butt on the field!"

I didn't know what to say. I took a deep breath and let it out slowly in an effort to gain control over my body. My mind raced. I knew I had to throw on the brakes. I had to stop thinking.

"Let go, Mohammad," I thought. "Just let go."

I approached the others. With the next step, I was on the field. With another step, I was in the scrimmage. In an instant, my body switched gears from fan to forward. The next thing I knew, I was racing up and down the field, making myself available for my team, which was in control of the ball. We raced toward the goal, and I was wide open for the pass. But it didn't come. We lost control of the ball for a moment, but then we regained it. Again, I was wide open, waiting for the pass.

"Am I invisible?" I thought.

The player took a risk and passed the ball to Naim. My cousin sped toward the goal, but two opponents were on him. Again, I was wide open. He shot the ball across the field to me. My feet propelled it toward the goal. Just as I was getting ready to pass it off, another player came and stole the ball from me. I was embarrassed.

But I made sure that the next time I had possession of the ball, I did not lose it. I passed the ball to a player near the goal. He sliced it in and scored our first point.

"Yes!" I thought.

My bones and muscles danced inside my skin.

The game continued. It was obvious to me that, while I didn't have the level of skill that the other players had, I had speed and agility. After a while, others started to pass the ball to me. I assisted two more goals and made another one on my own.

"Why don't you start practicing with us?" Naim said after the game.

"Are you sure?" I asked.

"Of course, I'm sure," he said. "You probably won't get to play much in the beginning, but, with a little practice, I think you'll be as good as our senior players in no time. What do you say?"

"Sure, buddy," I said. "I mean ... yes. Of course!"

"All right then," he said. "See you tomorrow at four o'clock."

After that, I practiced from four to six o'clock, three to four days a week with Bamica, and every other day with the school team. That schedule on top of my schoolwork was rough, but my body and mind were so elated that they handled the schedule with ease. My main challenge was to continually invent excuses for leaving the house early or returning late.

All of my trees died that year.

* * *

"Father, here. Let me do that for you," I said, reaching for his shovel. Father and one of his friends stood in the yard where he had selected the spot for a new tree.

"No, Mohammad," he said. "That's all right. Run along now. Find something else to do."

"Come on," Father's friend said. "Let him have the shovel. He's young. He could do it in half the time."

"That boy has poison on his hands. Everything he touches dies," Father said. "It's more than bad luck. It's a curse. They're cursed poisonous hands, and I don't want them anywhere near this tree."

"Father, please," I said. "I am only going to touch the shovel and dig the hole for you. I won't even touch the tree. What can go wrong?"

I spent the next five minutes pleading with him to let me do the work for him.

"The boy is right," Father's friend said. "What can go wrong?"

"All right. All right. Here," Father said, handing me the shovel.

I took the shovel and aimed its blunt blade into the ground. I lifted my bare foot and stepped down as hard as I could to break the dry dirt below. The blade hit the earth. Snap! The shovel's handle split in two. Immensely embarrassed, I looked up at Father.

"I don't know what happened, I just—" I started to say.

"See," Father said, turning to his friend, "I told you that the boy has poison on his hands. How long have I used that shovel without breaking it?

Go on, Mohammad. Get out of here. I don't want to see you anywhere near my garden again. And I'll be reassigning your trees."

Being relieved of my duty to care for trees forced me to become creative with my excuses to leave for practice, but there were only so many times I could say, "It's too noisy here. I'm going to walk around and work on memorization."

From time to time, Father would approach Mother about my absence.

"You know he has to study more than the others," she would say to him.

That usually satisfied his curiosity. Then my ally would come and warn me to be careful.

"I don't even know why you are doing this, *Bad-bakht*," Mother said on numerous occasions.

Upon hearing "*Bad-bakht*," the little boy inside me would jump up and down and scream, "I am not *Bad-bakht*! I am not! I am not! I am not! You'll see! You'll see one day!"

Rather than let the little boy express himself, I turned his anger into determination and calmly replied, "If I want to play for the national team, I've got to do it."

"Oh, Mohammad," she said. "Stop dreaming such big things. You've got to be realistic."

I'd hear that a lot in life.

* * *

I practiced hard during my first year on the team. Soon, my skill caught up with my speed. The next thing I knew, I was starting my ninth-grade year and received an invitation to play for the national youth team. Mother was proud, but she remained skeptical of my ultimate goal. Father remained unaware.

My status as a *Bamica* team player and national youth team player boosted my social immunity. It served as a wall of protection that surrounded me everywhere I went. The gangs and bullies at school and in the city overlooked me instead of taunting me or inviting me to join their antics. I felt on top of the world in Kabul.

Despite the fact that life in Kabul was going well for me and my family hadn't returned to Saikanda for a couple of winters, a part of my heart was still in that village.

*   *   *

Tenth grade meant it was time for me to start thinking about my future and what I wanted to do after high school. Although I wanted to be a soccer player more than anything, I knew I couldn't be one forever and I should follow in my oldest brother's footsteps and go to college. Abdul Mateen was the first in our family to attend college, and Father was very proud of him.

*   *   *

"Mohammad," Father said to me one day. "Have you given any thought to what you want to study at the university?"

"Yes, Father, I have," I said.

A part of me was excited to tell him of my plans, but most of me was nervous.

"Ah? Tell me," he said.

"I'd like to study medicine," I said. I partially expected what followed.

"Medicine?" he questioned. "Oh, child, you are crazier than I thought. What do you want to do? Kill everybody?"

"No, Father," I said. "I want to save lives. That's what doctors do."

On the outside, I was calm, but the little boy inside crossed his arms, tapped his foot, and scowled at his father.

"I know what doctors do," he said. "And I know what you do. You can't study medicine for two reasons. Number one, you aren't smart enough. Number two, you kill everything you touch. What does your mother call you? *Bad-bakht*?"

"I'll study hard, Father. You'll see," I said.

"I am not *Bad-bakht*!" the little boy screamed.

"Have you thought about business?" Father asked. "Your brother could help you."

*   *   *

I hadn't let Father's lack of belief in my abilities deter me before, and I wasn't about to let it deter me now. If nothing else, it fueled my drive to succeed. Sure, I had thought about being a businessman, as he had been once. Of course, I had thought about studying business. I grew up watching others respect and rely on Father to help them with their problems. Part of me wanted to be in the same position. I wanted to be the go-to man of Saikanda.

But I knew I wasn't business material, and Father should have known it, too. Where he was charismatic, I was awkward. Where he led, I assisted. Where he worked alone, I worked on a team. Rather than becoming another local businessman with all the answers, I decided to become the first local doctor in Saikanda.

Saikandans had never had a doctor live among them. When a villager became ill, others led him or her by donkey or carried the patient by foot to Mehtar-Lam. I had heard many stories about people dying on their way to the doctor's home. Simply by living in Saikanda, I knew I could help save lives. I dreamed of having a small office and trading business for eggs and bread or whatever my friends and neighbors could afford. In my own way, I would be filling Father's shoes by serving the village.

In reality, however, there wasn't much I would be able to do for the villagers. Their health problems were much more widespread and complex than a young boy could fathom. A single doctor among the village couldn't begin to solve those problems. Today, even the most advanced countries haven't figured out how to change the behavior of their population, behavior that could add years of quality life to the people.

Mother actually kept our family alive. In Saikanda, she woke up early every morning to have enough time to draw the water and boil it for us. When we lived in Kabul, she was one of the first people in line to receive *nal*, the term used for the government-supplied, iodine-treated water. She kept our drinking water clean, and she kept us clean. She drew our baths once every week or two, and she prompted us to wash our hands daily.

She didn't know what exactly, but she knew something was in the water. She knew it killed children by giving them diarrhea and nausea until their little bodies became so weak that they gave up and died.

She had held mothers as they mourned with empty arms for their dead children. Their inconsolable cries helped to give Mother the strength she needed, even though her aches and pains worsened as she walked to and from the well or stood in line every day.

"When is *nal* coming?" asked the women who knew that using iodine-treated water was better for health.

If the answer was six o'clock in the morning, Mother was there, thirty minutes ahead of time. In Kabul, the water only ran for two hours, and she wanted to make sure there was enough to fill her buckets. She walked to the designated spot and set down her buckets to claim her place in line. Then she visited the various markets and shopped until the tanks of *nal* came. After filling her buckets, she wrapped her gnarled fingers around the wire handles and carried them home. Once home, there was no time to rest as she started her work for the day.

* * *

"Mother, don't worry about me. I'll be fine," I said.

It was late in the summer. My tenth-grade year was nearing an end. I was, once again, trying to convince her that I didn't need a bath. Of course, she wouldn't have it any other way, so she drew the water and boiled it for me, as she did for everyone, though most of us could have done it ourselves with less hassle. She worked hard for our family. If nothing else, I wanted to make her proud of me. Being a doctor would do that.

So I gathered the strength to ask Father for the money I would need to stay in Kabul and take a preparation course that winter. He denied my first request. He told me that I was being ridiculous. He said that I'd never be able to be a success because I killed everything I touched.

He denied my second request. He told me that I'd never get into medical school anyway. To my third request, he responded that he didn't have the money. By the fourth request, the idea of having a doctor as a son had weakened his stance.

"Father, this is my dream. I can do this," I begged.

"Mohammad," he said. "I'm not sure if I'm about to make a good investment or the worst mistake of my life."

He stopped and looked at me. My heart raced in anticipation as he reached inside his jacket.

"I had to borrow this," Father said. He pulled the money I needed for the course out of his pocket and looked at me. "While there's a chance you can pull this off, I'm pretty sure you won't unless you stop hanging out with your friends so much and keep your head in the books. You can't waste time like you used to. You're not the brightest kid, Mohammad. You've got to remember how hard you worked to get to this point. You've got to understand how much harder you're going to have to work to succeed from here on out."

"Of course, Father," I said.

He went on for another ten minutes before handing me the money.

He finally said, "Now go pay for the course before you lose that."

Just as my plans to study medicine started to come together, *Bamica* started to fall apart, and I was caught in the middle. The better players split to form a team called *Hindokosh*, but my cousin stayed with the original team that he had formed. Both teams wanted me to join them. Unable to choose between my cousin and my friends, I quit altogether.

With the breakup of *Bamica* following the breakdown of Nasir, I was so depressed and distracted that I thought about ditching education altogether and showing Father that he was right about me all along.

If it wasn't for the encouragement of a few people I really respected and admired and was fortunate to know, I don't know if I would be where I am today. My cousin, Tahir Safi, gave me the emotional support for which I thirsted. He listened as I rambled on about the waste of an education.

"You can't sit there and tell me that, if I go to school now, I will be promised a better life in the future," I argued. "Look at Nasir. He went to school. He was smart. What's in his future?"

"Mohammad, you've got—" he started.

But I cut him off. "Nothing! That's what! Nothing is in his future. He's crazy."

Tahir Safi listened and nodded as I first talked about Nasir. Then I went on about the weaknesses of formal education.

"You have some good points, and you might be right. Humor me, Mohammad," he said. "What would you like to be doing ten years from now?"

"I'll be a player for the national team," I said.

Without laughing or telling me how impossible it would be to meet my goal, he simply nodded and said, "Okay, so you're on the national team. For some reason you have to quit or you get injured and you can't play anymore. Then what would you like to do next?"

"I'd like to be a doctor in Saikanda," I said. "I'd be the first one in our village."

"Medicine?" he said. "That's crazy. How does a soccer player have time to study medicine?"

His way was subtle. He asked just the right questions. Naïve and unaware of his strategy, I spent the next few minutes convincing him that my ability to read and memorize quickly would leave me plenty of time for soccer.

"It's the perfect plan, buddy. It takes advantage of all my talents," I said as I wrapped up my argument for my abilities to do both.

I continued to play for the youth soccer team, but I took a break from my complete focus on the sport for the next couple years. Instead, I concentrated all my efforts on my studies from grades ten to twelve. In addition to studying for high school exams, I studied to pass the entrance exam required for medical school. For months, I studied from 4 o'clock, starting after my classes, and then went until near dawn. Then I woke up after a couple hours of sleep and got ready for another day of school, soccer, and studying. In 1977, I graduated third in my class.

* * *

After a very tough entrance exam, I gained entrance into the University of Kabul in Afghanistan. I started medical school with a strong sense of purpose and energy. It was obvious to everyone that I was taking my studies and future very seriously. That sense of purpose, however, received a huge shock during the second month of my medical training.

* * *

On April 27, 1978, there was another coup. Our small communist party, which the Soviet Union strongly supported, captured and killed Mohammad Daud Khan. The nation's pulse came to a stop.

* * *

"*Bretylium,*" *I order again.*

I can see in the glance that she exchanges with the other nurse that she's considering gently suggesting again that I call the patient's time of death.

"*Five hundred milligrams IV over one minute,*" *I continue without pause,* "*and then start an infusion.*"

"*I have amiodarone,*" *she says.*

"*No, this is better,*" *I say, nodding toward the cart.*

I hope the bretylium is there. I have read that the only antiarrhythmic to show benefit in hypothermia was bretylium.

"*All right, buddies,*" *I say.* "*Let's keep the warm saline coming. She's not dead until she's warm and dead.*"

I hope I am right about the bretylium.

Chapter Seven:
Nightfall

When Daud established a democracy in Afghanistan, he promised to strengthen the country, both internally and externally. However, he executed his plans poorly and ruled without much input from other government representatives. While he did begin to reopen trade doors with Iran and Pakistan, he failed to follow through on his domestic agenda. The situation further deteriorated with his efforts to quiet dissenting groups, such as the growing number of fundamentalists and communists.

With each passing month, Afghans grew more disgruntled with the lack of improvements in their state and the many arrests, exiles, and executions that he ordered. Daud's popularity flatlined.

Soviet leaders noticed. They determined that, with a little encouragement and support, the People's Democratic Party of Afghanistan (PDPA) could take the reins of control from Daud. They helped the small party gain popularity by encouraging and supporting demonstrations against the unpopular president.

On April 19, 1978, Nur Muhammad Taraki, Hafizullah Amin, and Babrak Karmal leveraged the death of *Parcham* member Mir Akbar Khyber, the most recent and beloved in a string of political figures to be assassinated, to rally tens of thousands to their cause.

The already paranoid Daud took action against the three PDPA figures. He put Taraki in prison and placed Amin under house arrest. Karmal had enough time to leave the country and seek shelter in the Soviet Union.

On April 27, the PDPA initiated a coup d'état. Many say Amin commanded the coup by passing orders through family members who visited him in the confines of his own home. On April 28, a new government took control of the country. The new regime announced that Daud resigned due to health conditions. The truth slowly emerged. Rebels had killed Daud, along with some of his family members, in the presidential palace.

Although the *Khalq* and *Parcham* factions appeared to be united under the leadership of the newly established president, Taraki, who was released from prison following Daud's death, and the new deputy prime minister, Amin, conflict continued. Behind the scenes, Taraki and Amin, both *Khalqi*, remained the staunch enemies of Babrak Karmal, who had returned from the Soviet Union, and Muhammad Najibullah, both *Parchami* leaders.

As soon as Taraki gained control, he implemented a ten o'clock curfew for the entire nation. He also established laws that changed marriage and funeral proceedings. Many Afghans, being as steeped in tradition about such personal ceremonies as most cultures, disregarded or misunderstood the changes, which resulted in numerous arrests and deaths. Widespread changes to laws governing land ownership unsettled many people. Confusion set in throughout Afghanistan.

The changes, designed to weaken cultural and religious beliefs and suppress pride and courage, were supposed to replace our old nationalistic and religious identity with Communist ideals. For some, however, the changes only ignited rebellious sentiments. An antigovernment movement slowly emerged, initiated by those who the new laws affected. Because most of the initial acts against our culture affected our freedoms to speak, think for, and express ourselves, the well-educated among us comprised a large majority of the first wave of people to speak out against the government. This group included many of my fellow university students.

* * *

"What the hell is going on?" Shafi asked as we sat at a teahouse near the university.

"Shh," Tashir said. He flashed his eyes around at the crowd.

"All right. I'll be quiet," Shafi said. "You don't have to be so paranoid. These are university people. They know what's going on. You can trust them."

"I wouldn't be so sure about that," I said. "You can't trust your best friends these days."

I told them about Father's friend and distant relative, Ghulam Nabi. Father had cared for Nabi most of his life and treated him like a son. They were very close, but, as soon as the Communist party gained control, Nabi viewed Father as a wealthy man, even though he had been wealthy only once and was now poor again. Nabi saw Father as an enemy. He wouldn't even say hello to him anymore. Their broken trust shook Father to the core.

"I'm telling you, buddy," I said. "You don't really know who you can trust these days."

"You can trust me," Shafi said.

We laughed.

"I mean it," he said.

"Yeah, man, we know," Yahya said.

Of course, we trusted Shafi. He was the most outspoken one among us. If his sentiments had changed, his uncensored passion would have revealed that, probably in the form of a poem.

"So I'll see you guys tonight, right?" he asked.

"I'll be there." I said. "What about you?"

I looked around the table at the others. Satar and Tashir said they had to be somewhere else.

"I wouldn't miss it," Yahya said. "You're going to read, right?"

"Of course," said Shafi. "What do you expect?"

Shafi certainly had a way with words. He often cloaked jabs at the government so well that the audience thought he was opening a window to his soul and baring the scars of unrequited love. Those of us who knew him, however, sat in awe at the hidden meanings veiled in his clever prose.

* * *

As the months passed, the sharing of antigovernment sentiments cost people more than friendships and close ties with family members. Eventually, one didn't know who actually worked as a mole, combing his or her acquaintances and fellow citizens for traitors to turn in to the secret police.

In an effort to quiet the antigovernment movement, the new regime started to arrest anybody who spoke out against its ideas. They sometimes killed people without a trial in order to reinforce the point to others. As friend turned in friend, my countrymen and women started to look over their shoulders.

Desperation fueled the movement, which originated in Kabul, where government control was the strongest, into the surrounding, more rural, regions. Yelling, retaliation, and riots became common. Later, the hollow sounds of bullets, machine-gun fire, and rocket explosions replaced lullabies as families huddled together at night for a sense of security. It all became as natural a part of evening as the fall of darkness. Eventually, when we didn't hear the sounds of fighting, we thought something was gravely wrong.

* * *

"They're forgetting that this isn't normal," Shafi said.

We weren't sitting in the teahouse that day. We were at Shafi's place. Now, even he wanted to make sure that nobody overheard us.

"We've got to do something," he said as he agitatedly paced the floor, wringing his hands in much the same way Nasir had done during his madness.

This was normal for Shafi though. He couldn't sit still, and he couldn't keep quiet. His soul boiled with words.

"Did your friend get back to you?" Yahya asked.

"Not yet," Shafi said. "Not yet. But he will. And when he does …"

His words trailed off as he felt around in his pants pockets. His eyes popped wide when he found the object of his search. He pulled it from his pocket, unfolded what would become an underground newspaper with both hands, and snapped it open before us.

He held it up and said, "*Shabnama.*"

"*Shabnama,*" I said. "I like the sound of that."

"Night News," Tahir said. "Appropriate. We'll want to keep it very quiet. No one can know what we're doing."

"The nights aren't so quiet these days," said Yahya. "We'll have to be very careful." He stared at Tahir.

"The word 'night' refers more to the veil that is being drawn over our country, the darkness that enshrouds Afghans," Shafi said. "It's up to us to spread a small light of remembrance. I want everyone who reads this to remember that this is not our Afghanistan and it's up to us to keep in mind who we truly are and take back our country."

* * *

During the year-and-a-half that Taraki ruled Afghanistan, tensions within the government burned red-hot. Taraki had attempted to get rid of Karmal and other *Parchami* leaders by assigning them to positions abroad, eventually arresting, exiling, or killing them. When Karmal started to fear that his life was in danger, he left Afghanistan and returned to the Soviet Union.

* * *

On December 5, 1978, Taraki signed a friendship treaty with the Soviet Union. In March 1979, Taraki invited Soviet troops to support his fight against the attacks of tribal-based freedom fighters called *mujahideen* (strugglers).

Taraki also decided to step up control within his party. With the encouragement of Soviet Leader Leonid Ilyich Brezhnev, he plotted to have Amin killed. But Amin escaped the shootout unharmed. He returned to the palace. With the help of a guard, he captured and killed Taraki on September 14, 1979.

The media reported that Taraki had died of a serious chronic disease. Months later, the public would learn that Amin had delivered the orders to end Taraki's life by smothering him with a pillow.

As soon as he came to power, the new president turned on his own *Khalqui* party. Amin figuratively placed a pillow over the mouths of his fellow PDPA members with the execution of thousands. Amin became more nationalistic and tried to gain popular support by restoring religious freedoms and promoting Islam in speeches and at meetings. He became friendlier to Pakistan, which was allied with the United States, and started calling for war against Iran.

The Soviet Union realized Amin was drifting toward the West and became concerned about his allegiance, especially because he had once studied in the United States. Eventually, Amin refused to heed Soviet advice. Soviet leaders were not pleased. Afghans certainly were not pleased. They were petrified.

Amin may have turned to Islam to try to win back support, but he turned away from the teachings of peace that form the core of the religion. He instead used his power to persecute perceived enemies and start down the path toward ethnic cleansing.

His brief tenure as president was brutal, fanning the flames of angry fear throughout the nation. On December 26, 1979, fear knocked at my door.

* * *

I was living with Abdul Mateen, who stayed in Kabul to work at his government job, and Nadir, who was studying economics, for the winter. My brothers and I confined ourselves to one room of the house because we could only afford to keep one woodstove burning. That evening was especially cold. We sat around the fire, passing around a bowl of *shorwa* (a lamb and carrot soup).

A rapid knock fired at the door.

"Who could that be?" Abdul Mateen asked as he got up to answer.

Nadir and I stared at each other, not moving or breathing. Abdul Mateen hesitated for a moment before he opened the door. The knock came again. This time, it was louder, more insistent, and more rapid.

I bit my lip as my brother opened the door.

Standing in our doorway was a tall, thin figure wrapped in an Arab cloak. His blue eyes searched the room and landed on mine.

"Mohammad," the man said.

"Yahya," I said as I rose to meet him. "Are you all right? Come in. Is everything okay?"

"No. They're coming to get me," he said.

"Who?" Nadir asked.

"The soldiers," he said. "Tonight."

"Are you serious? How do you know?" I asked my best friend, even though I knew the answer.

Yahya's cousin, Adeeb, worked for the government. He had been flaunting his power in front of others for weeks, taunting Yahya and his family that he was going to turn them in just because he could. No one doubted that Adeeb's word alone would get the family arrested and maybe even killed. With each passing December day, the stories of arrest and execution piled higher than the snow.

"Can I stay here tonight?" he asked.

"Stay as long as you need to," I said, turning to Nadir and Abdul Mateen for confirmation.

Yahya joined us as we returned to the fire's warm embrace. We drank chai, a type of tea, and listened to his account of the rumors that had prompted his family to flee their home in search of shelter. Too depressed for conversation, we sat around and listened to the crackle and hiss of the burning wood.

Just before midnight, we each rose to say the last of five prayers that Muslims recite each day. We hadn't always prayed, but we did pray more during those frightening times. Then we sat around and forced idle chatter as we played cards.

"What was that?" Yahya asked.

"What?"

"Listen," he said. "They're coming."

The next thing we knew, the popcorn sounds of machine guns broke the evening's silence. We dropped our cards and threw our bodies flat against the floor.

"I'm sorry," Yahya said. "I'm sorry."

"Be quiet!" Abdul Mateen snapped.

A storm of jets flew over our home. They seemed to crisscross the sky all over the city. We didn't know what was going on. We just lay there, listening to the symphony of destruction that banged on the instruments of war surrounding our home. Abdul Mateen moved carefully, but he only went to turn on the radio.

Four hours later, Karmal's voice announced over the radio, "Amin is out of power. The murderer, the dictator, is no longer in control. I am here now, and I am your president."

The sounds of cheering lured us outdoors from our warm abode. Everyone in my neighborhood was outside. They yelled in jubilation from their rooftops, terraces, and porches. I looked around at the men, women, and children rejoicing in unity. For the first time in a long time, I felt hope for my country. Yahya's face broke into a smile.

"I can't believe it," he said. His words turned into hysterical laughter as he realized what this meant for his cousin's threats. "It's a dream come true."

But the next morning, the dream was shattered, and the nightmare began.

Chapter Eight:
Testing Culture

The next morning, my heart and body were exhausted and wanted—or rather needed—the rejuvenation from sleep. My consciousness was caught in a battle between the faded fictions of slumber and the low-frequency noises that rumbled in the ground beneath me. I tossed and turned. A rumble came, tugged at my mind, nudged it, and dragged it to the surface. I opened my eyes. I looked around. The rumble was gone. The others were still sleeping. It was dark. I put my head back down and immediately fell asleep. Another rumble came, tempting my mind to surface. This time, it worked.

"Huh!" I said, lifting my head and looking around.

I was a swimmer emerging breathlessly from dark waters. It was lighter outside, but I felt darker.

"Where's Yahya?" I wondered, looking around until my unfocused eyes found him sleeping by the fire.

"Everyone is safe. Everything is fine," I whispered inside my mind as I recalled the memories from the night before.

I put down my head and tried to fall asleep again. This time, I couldn't. I was too nervous. A different sound came. While straining my ears to listen, I recognized the muffled voices in an argument. I couldn't make out the words.

Pop! Pop! Pop! Pop! Pop! Pop! Pop!

The others awoke, startled.

"What was that?" Yahya asked. He sat up from the floor, stiff as a wax figure. His eyes darted from side to side like the bird in a cuckoo clock. But he was not alarming anyone. He was the alarmed one.

"It's a little early for celebrating," Nadir said, rolling over and covering his cold ears with his hands.

"I don't think that was celebration," Abdul Mateen said. He stood up and walked to the door. "You guys stay here."

But we disobeyed and followed him.

"What the …?" My brother's words fell out of his mouth and landed on the frozen earth beneath our bare feet.

We didn't move.

"What's going on?" Nadir asked. "What the hell is that guy doing?" He referred to the armed, uniformed man sitting on top of a grey-green tank in the distance. The soldier held a long gun in his hands. The big, furry hat atop his head moved back and forth as he looked up and down the streets.

It wasn't long before we learned that Soviet tanks didn't just stand watch in our neighborhood. The metal beasts loomed in every street and alley of Kabul. Foreigners held their leashes, and these people would reveal themselves as a new, deadly breed of bullies.

* * *

"They're just here to keep everybody quiet and enforce the curfew," Yahya said a couple weeks later as we walked down the hallway of the university building to our classroom. "Karmal wants to make sure that things go well during his transition into power. That's all."

"How is it—" I started.

"Shh," Shafi interrupted as we passed a group of *Parcham* members.

We exchanged greetings with our fellow soccer teammates and then turned to enter our classroom.

"How is it," I whispered, "that death is a proper punishment for breaking curfew?"

Yahya was careful in his judgments as well as in his actions. He didn't want to believe that the regime change, which he had thanked for saving his life, could be responsible for the deaths of others. But it was hard to ignore the stories. Only two weeks ago, they had breezed in and out lightly from time to time. Now, they gusted daily.

"Anyway," I said as we took our seats in the front of the class, "you are meeting with us tonight, right?"

"Yes, of course," he replied. "Look, Mohammad … I know what's going on. It's just hard. That's all."

"Yeah, I know. That's why we've got to do this." I finished my sentence just as the professor stepped up to the podium to begin his lecture about bacteria identification.

* * *

It's hard to identify bacteria just by looking at them. Even under a fine microscope lens, different bacteria appear similar. Therefore, scientists provide pieces from one sample bacteria in an array of cultures. When bacteria are in their preferred home, in this case, a petri dish, they thrive. Therefore, if a bacteria sample flourishes in an environment without oxygen, scientists know the bacteria are anaerobic. Thus, they can rule out all bacteria that require oxygen to live, and they can pursue further identification based on other attributes.

Around Kabul and all over the country, a few individuals, who previously had been isolated in their beliefs, started banding together for a cause. They called themselves *mujahideen* (freedom fighters).

Under normal circumstances, the violent mind-set that required *mujahideen* to turn on their own neighbors would have been rare in Afghanistan. But under the new circumstances, that is, the new culture that had been forced upon us, the mind-set flourished.

The culture of oppression is an excellent petri dish for growing rebels. If you add monetary and weapons support from Western countries, that culture promotes cancerous growth.

* * *

I left for Shafi's house around six o'clock. The streets were almost clear. Although the curfew wouldn't take effect for another four hours, people stopped leaving their homes after dusk, fearing something terrible would keep them from returning in time or maybe not at all.

It was cold outside. As I walked toward his home, my whole body stiffened, but it wasn't entirely because of the weather. Every time I turned a corner, I approached the menacing silhouette of a tank or an armed soldier. I'd sometimes see both. My chest held my dry breath tightly while my right hand pressed a piece of paper flat inside my pants pocket as I passed each checkpoint.

Trying to appear as if I was too freezing cold to notice the presence of the tanks and soldiers, I looked straight ahead as if I was almost in sight of my warm home. It worked. No one stopped me or even said a word to me that night. I turned the final corner in my journey, relieved to see that the street was clear. I quickened my pace until I reached the front door of Shafi's home.

I let out a deep sigh, removed my hand from my pants pocket, and raised it to knock at the door.

Just before my knuckles tapped on the door, I heard footsteps. I froze. My jaw locked tightly. The steps slowed and then stopped right behind me. I couldn't swallow. I couldn't breathe. I slowly turned around.

"Hey," said a tired voice. "Whoa! You okay? What? Did you think I was a soldier?"

"Hey, Tahir," I said, exhaling the cloudy breath I had been holding. "Were you stopped?"

"No," he said. "You?"

"No," I said.

A few minutes later, we—along with Yahya and Sameem—were huddled in a corner of Shafi's home.

"Did you bring them?" Shafi asked.

He set down his teacup and opened his hands to us. Sameem and I pulled out pieces of paper from our pockets. Tahir took one from under his hat. Yahya sat down on the floor to retrieve the one he had carried in his shoe.

"What?" he asked as we stared at him. "I like to be careful."

"Yeah, we know," Shafi said, collecting the contributions to *Shabnama*. He placed the papers in the middle of a textbook, closed it, and stuffed it deep into his backpack. "I'll be able to get this to the printer tomorrow. On Thursday, I'll deliver copies to Mohammad. Then he'll get them to each of you. Okay?"

We agreed and picked up our cups to finish drinking the lukewarm tea.

"So, ah, who is this guy with the printer?" Tahir asked.

"He prefers not to be known," Shafi said. "Why do you care anyway?"

"I care because we're doing business with him," Tahir said. "How do we know we can trust him?"

"Do you trust me?" asked Shafi.

"Well, yeah, but—" started Tahir.

"Do you or don't you want to be a part of this?" snapped Shafi.

"Of course, I do, but there's a lot at stake here. I just want to know if we can trust him," said Tahir.

"Look, Tahir," Shafi said, his voice softening. He sighed. "If I'm the only one who meets with him, then I'm the only one he can incriminate."

Tahir nodded. The discussion was over.

We spent the rest of our time dividing the campus and venues and deciding who would be responsible for each of the territories.

I left Shafi's home well before ten o'clock. I was a little more confident since I was no longer carrying the incriminating antigovernment article that I had written.

* * *

Unlike the *mujahideen*, who waged war against the enemy, we students battled the complacency of our own people. Our words traveled from shadow to shadow as we handed out *Shabnama* all over campus. Yahya and I usually worked together. One of us would take a seat at a table while the other went into the bathroom and left copies of our newsletter. We left them on tables, in chairs, and on benches. We left them anywhere we thought people might find them.

The headlines read:

"Babrak Is a Puppet!"

"Soviets Pull Strings."

"This Is Not My Afghanistan."

Our reporting wasn't mind-blowing, but it focused us. It gave us a sense of power and purpose when everything around us was falling apart.

* * *

Over the next week, rumors from a few became reality for many. The stories that traveled from ear to ear in the morning were backed up by screams and gunfire the night before. Not only did the Communist regime continue to inflict cruelties upon us, but such incidents increased in frequency and severity. In just a few weeks, soldiers had created new ways to use their unchecked power to their advantage. I heard a lot of stories like this one:

"Did you hear about what happened to the Khans? All the children had just fallen asleep when two big soldiers banged on their door. Almost broke it down."

"What? Why?"

"Who knows why? They saw a room filled with eight children. Only one was a boy. One of the men walked over, dragged the boy up by his collar, and put a gun to his head. He threatened to take him away if the family didn't give them all of their money."

"All of their money? But they're poor as dirt."

"Isra gathered the girls together as Jamal emptied his pockets and money jars. He gave them what few rupees he could gather. He then scrambled about the house and gathered everything of value that he could find. What else could they do? Otherwise, the soldier would have arrested him and taken him to prison."

"On what charge? He's just a boy."

"Does it matter? Everyone knows a soldier's testimony is good enough for a conviction and a lifetime sentence to Pol-e-Charkhi."

Another familiar story went like this:

"He was the ugliest, dirtiest, forty-year-old man they'd ever seen. Hardly had a tooth in his mouth. The smell? Yuck! They said his breath smelled of rotten eggs and fish."

"And Laila's father gave his permission? She was only fifteen years old and so beautiful!"

"Of course, he did. He had to. The soldier threatened that, if he couldn't have her as his bride, he would rape her. Then who would want her? It's so sad."

"To think, that beautiful girl is now stuck with that beast of a man for the rest of her life."

"No, she's not. It gets worse. The whole neighborhood woke up that night when they heard her mother's scream. It pierced through every barrier when she found her daughter lying on the floor covered in blood."

"She took her own life?"

"She sneaked into the kitchen, took a sharp knife from a table, and killed herself right there in the next room. Her father and the soldier were arguing so much that nobody heard her body fall. She might as well have killed her mother along with herself. The poor woman hasn't stopped wailing in three full days."

From what I could gather, these were not isolated events. Stories like this (and far worse) regularly traveled from ear to ear and from neighborhood to neighborhood.

Eventually, the terrible shots and screams that sounded back and forth throughout the night spilled into the day. Without the veil of darkness, the nighttime atrocities were revealed. And they weren't all the doings of oppressors.

* * *

As part of a wedding custom in our culture, a groom slaughters a rooster and wipes its blood on his bride's shoes before she enters their home. The groom then hands the slaughtered animal to their wedding driver.

Much later in my life, when I married my wife, I couldn't gather the strength to go through with the custom. I dumbfounded my family when I handed our driver a live rooster and my wife entered our home without bloodstained shoes. According to Mother, the fate of her "unlucky one" was decided. I didn't stand a chance after that.

I couldn't bring myself to kill an animal that I didn't need to eat. It's in my nature that I can't stand violence. But, one day, I found myself face-to-face with it.

* * *

The morning was so cold that I dreaded leaving my home. I thought of Saikanda, and I longed to be there. There, it was warmer, and I could visit with Anwar. I'd much rather be pouring tea than poring over books all night. My memories of him, however, seemed like they belonged to another person and another life altogether. So much had changed. My purpose was no longer the search and conquest of rupees and treats or rides on a donkey. I shook off my warm childhood memories and braced myself for the cold that waited for me on the other side of the door.

"Where are you going?" Father asked. I was about to leave.

"To study with Yahya," I said, turning to look at him.

He could tell I was lying. I had lied to him so many times before. This time, it was so close to the truth that he didn't believe me.

"Yeah?" he asked. "Well, be careful."

"Yes, Father, I will," I said.

His dark eyes captured me. They embraced me. In a look, they said the words I hadn't heard in years. I couldn't move. For the first time in a long time, I felt his love for me. But it was more than that. I felt his concern for me.

"Thank you," I said.

"And stay warm," he added. "Good thing you've got all that crazy hair on a day like today."

I left our fire-warmed home and shut the door behind me. Just before putting on my hat, I ruffled my hair with my fingers. Somewhere deep inside of me, a little boy smiled.

That morning, just a few weeks after Babrak stepped up to the pulpit of power, I was on my way to meet Yahya to work on an article for *Shabnama*. I folded my arms against my chest, looked down, and started on the path that I could have walked with my eyes closed.

After a couple of blocks of saying "excuse me" and bumping shoulders with others, I looked up and realized I was trying to cut through a huge stream of people. It looked like everyone in town was making their way through the streets toward the city center. I followed.

I spotted Farid, the neighbor who had helped organize our soccer games when I was young, in front of me.

"Hey, what's going on?" I asked.

"Man, where've you been, Mohammad?" he asked. "A demonstration is gathering."

My legs stopped taking the long strides required to keep up with my childhood hero. I stood there and watched hundreds of people walk past me. Ahead of me, in the distance, the crowd started chanting.

"Down with Babrak!"

"Down with the puppet!"

The soldiers around me snapped into sniper mode. Their hawkish eyes scoped for prey. Rather than talons, these predators wielded machine guns, which they pointed at the men, women, and children who marched by in the streets. They were ready to kill.

Then the people around me chimed in.

"Down with Babrak!"

"Down with the puppet!"

I needed to swallow, but couldn't. For a second, I thought I was going to choke on my own spit and die right there. My death would not have been by the hands of foreigners, but by my own fear, as it coiled its snakelike body around my neck. I tugged at my throat with my finger, made room to breathe, and started walking.

The pace quickened. The purpose became urgent.

"Down with Babrak!"

"Down with the puppet!"

To get a better view of what was going on, I moved to the outside of the street. From there, I could see what had been hidden. I felt around in my pockets, but they were empty.

"Down with Babrak!"

"Down with the puppet!"

Despite the constant threat of danger, I wasn't carrying a weapon. Even years after the invasion, I still didn't carry a weapon. Many of my friends and family always carried a weapon or a piece of wood, broken glass, or scrap metal somewhere on their persons. This was the day the weapons came out. The few who didn't have them raised their fists high above their heads and beat the air as they chanted.

"Down with Babrak!"

"Down with the puppet!"

When I arrived at the city center, a speaker stood above the crowd. Holding a megaphone to his lips, he called for Babrak to remove the soldiers from our corners and allow our children to play again and dream of a positive future. The crowd roared. The calls to action and the responding cheers volleyed back and forth for hours. Then the crowd erupted in violence.

A man with a beard caught my eye as he picked up a stick, held it with both hands, and smashed a car window. Then he pushed off from the pavement with both legs and jumped onto the hood of a car. His transformation had begun. A moment before, he was just another protester. Then, lifting his head, he yelled at the top of his lungs, looking like half-man and half-beast. A soldier fired bullets into the air. The man/beast jumped down from the car and got into a fight. He screamed as he knocked out all the windows of the car and raised his stick into the air. The transformation was complete. He was a beast, a slave to his passion. A soldier opened fire. The man/beast fell to the ground.

I watched as the blood pooled around him. I looked around at the crowd. No one else had noticed. They—adults and children alike—were too consumed by their own passionate anger to see what was happening around them. They wielded their weapons against the buildings and cars in the city center. More shots rang out. Soldiers marched toward the crowd. I turned to leave. Tears came from my eyes as the screams and gunfire erupted behind me.

I walked home as quickly as I could. After the last member of our family entered the house that night, we sighed with relief. We were all there. We sat together for comfort as guns fired throughout the night. Mother was the only one who walked around. She paced from room to room as she took inventory of our supplies.

"This isn't good," she said to Father as she sat down to comfort the smaller children. Her instinct, as usual, was dead-on.

* * *

Orders came the next morning.

"Stay indoors. Anyone caught outside will be killed."

That day was eerily quiet. Every once in a while, gunfire broke up the silence, but it always returned, leaving us no clue as to what was happening around us. The minutes ticked by slowly.

The next day was spent in much the same way. Mother served us carrots for breakfast, lunch, and dinner.

"Again?" Obaidullah asked.

"Be thankful we have food," Father said.

"And wood," Mother added.

I looked over at the fireplace. There was barely enough wood for another day. But I didn't worry. I knew Mother would find a way to make her fire burn. Not knowing how long we'd be locked up inside our home and being extra careful, Mother had stopped using the fire to keep warm. She was only using it for cooking. She handed me my bowl, which was lighter than it had been the night before. We were saving food, too.

After dinner, I retreated to my own little corner of the house and picked up a book. On the outside, I looked as if I was studying. On the inside, I was supplicating. I begged God to bring harmony, peace, law, and order to Afghanistan. I prayed until tears streamed down my face. In the end, I begged at least for the curfew to be lifted and for life to return to normal. Part of my prayer was answered. Two days later, the curfew was lifted, but life was far from normal.

* * *

On the fourth day after the riot, we emerged from our homes. The guards were gone.

"Is this the calm before the storm?" I wondered.

As we visited and checked on neighbors, we slowly discovered that every household had suffered a loss. From what we heard, thousands of people had been killed on the night of the riot. Almost the entire city of Kabul mourned as families sneaked out, searching for gravesites for their loved ones.

I walked around the neighborhood, listening to the cries and wails that came from within each house that I passed. I felt helpless, but my brother soon put an end to that.

"Mohammad," Abdul Mateen called, running up to me. "Follow me. We need your help."

"What's going on?" I asked.

"Ihsan," my brother said, swallowing. "He's dead."

"What?" I asked.

It was hard to fathom that he was dead. As much as we admired Farid for his soccer skills, we admired Ihsan for his spirit. He was always available to help anybody with anything. And he and his wife were one of the only couples I knew who were truly in love. Much like Nasir and Najiba's youthful romance, Ihsan and his wife were crazy about each other. They also used to sneak away and dream of a life together, but they had not been dealt the blow that had sent my brother over the edge. They'd received permission to marry.

The couple had brought great joy to both families with the announcement of the birth of a child. Their daughter was only one year old when her father was killed.

"He was on his way to check on his mother," my brother said as we walked, "when a bullet struck him. I don't know if it was intentional or not. It hit him in the chest. Probably killed him instantly."

We kept walking until we came upon a small circle of people. Their dark clothes stood out against the snow.

I'll never forget how well Ihsan wore death. He was a fair-skinned Afghan with light eyes and hair. Perhaps that's why his face didn't shock me as much as others had. He looked peaceful. Even his wife said so as she kissed his face one last time.

"Where will we bury him?" I asked. "There are so many fresh graves."

"We found a place by the mosque," Father said. "There weren't any soldiers there when I found it. We'd better go before someone else takes it."

We picked up the body and carried it through the snow to our neighborhood mosque. Except for the gravesites that scattered the earth, the ground was white that day. We set down the body, cleared the snow, and picked up our shovels.

* * *

The doors to our schools and offices opened again. People slowly started to return to their world, but nothing after the riot and citywide house arrest was ever the same. We lived in a new culture, a culture of fear. And, in this dish, both the *mujahideen* and the regime that had created this terror continued to flourish.

Chapter Nine:
Between the Lines

The riot sealed the lid on the glass jar in which we lived. We were trapped. There are three things one can do when trapped: fight, flee, or forget.

* * *

"Damn it," I said. "They'll probably fill his position with a communist. Heck, they might as well fill it with a soldier."

"It was bound to happen," said Yahya. "Professor Morad's family was rich, so they could afford to leave."

"If the smartest and most educated people keep leaving the country," Shafi said, "there won't be anyone left to rebuild it."

"Rebuild?" Yahya asked. "This isn't going to destroy us."

"Where have you been? Look around. It's happening. In the end, we may not be completely destroyed, but it will get worse before it gets better," predicted Shafi.

It was rare that our poet friend resorted to clichés, but he was one of few people who could repeat our society's most-parroted phrases with a spine-tingling resonance.

"What are they supposed to do then?" Yahya asked. "Sit around and watch? Maybe even die when they have the chance to leave? There's nothing for them here. I'd leave if I could."

"But here—our country—is where the fight is," Shafi said rather intensely.

"Fight? Not everyone is a fighter," Yahya said. "Certainly not Morad. He taught because he couldn't bear to work in the hospital any longer. What was he supposed to do? Join the *mujahideen*? Or switch parties and join the army?"

"They don't have to pick up guns to fight," Shafi said. He had recaptured his serenity for a moment, but then it was gone, submerged once more by passion. "They can fight the numbness. Like we are. They can fight the forgetfulness that is engulfing our people." He took out a wrinkled piece of paper from his pocket and stretched it out before us. "This. This is our weapon. This."

"Put that thing away," Yahya said, referring to a copy of the newsletter we had just finished handing out as discreetly as possible.

Shafi folded it up again and slipped it into his pocket. Yahya leaned back into his chair and sighed. His fatigue showed on his face in his eyes and mouth.

"Are we fighting?" he asked. "We're doing all this work. But for what? With a gun, at least I'd know if I had shot someone, but with this newsletter …"

"Yes," Shafi said, "we are fighting."

"Come on, Shafi," said Yahya. "We're handing out pieces of paper. We don't even have the guts to place them in people's hands anymore. We leave them around, hoping someone will pick them up. How do we know we're not tricking ourselves into feeling like we're doing something? For all we know, nobody reads them."

"We know," I said, rejoining the conversation.

Half of my mind was listening. My friends turned to me. I nodded across the room to the two men, who had been occupying the other half of my mind.

I noticed them initially because one man was very short and the other was very tall. Their silhouettes grabbed my attention from the periphery of my eyesight when they emerged from the restroom. I watched their eyes scan the teahouse. When the taller man's gaze found mine, I pretended to look around the room. Luckily, my eyes fell upon a friend, and we waved in recognition.

I watched the odd men walk over to the corner and sit down. The taller one unfolded a piece of paper he had been hiding in his left hand. Both read it. I waited for their expressions to tell me what they thought or where they stood. But they were good at hiding their feelings. Much like me (or I at least assumed I was that good), they didn't give any indication to which side of the line they belonged. Instead, they appeared to be sitting on, above, or somewhere in the middle. Maybe they were even unaware of sides. Perhaps like them, my closest friends knew my allegiance, but, to the rest of the world, I was neither black nor white. I was somewhere in between.

"Oh, come on," Yahya said. "How can you possibly know what they're thinking? They could be trying to find the people who left it behind. They could be spies."

"They're not spies," Shafi said.

"They might be," I said. "We just don't know."

We didn't know anymore. Ever since the riot, Babrak changed tactics. Rather than have a soldier on every corner, he spaced them out, which seemed to appease the people a little. But what we didn't know hurt us. Babrak had turned his attention to filling the ranks of the *Khad*, a government organization of spies and specially trained killers.

Most *Khad* members were trained in Russia to listen for the slightest whispers of antigovernment sentiments. They captured anyone they believed to be against them. They would torture, jail, or kill them. New stories of people that the *Khad* captured during the previous night trickled into everyone's rapidly growing grapevine every morning. The *Khad* often performed its arrests at night while people were asleep in their homes. Sometimes, a whole neighborhood would awaken to the screams and shouts of children as agents carried away a parent or sibling, who usually was never seen again.

"No, we don't know for sure what they think or what anyone else thinks or if Shabnama even changes any minds," Shafi said. "But we've got to keep trying. We may not be picking up guns or blowing up bridges like the *mujahideen*, but we are fighting. In the end, our fight will be more important. If we don't win the battle against our own forgetfulness of how Afghanistan used to be, then we'll become our own monster, a monster without culture or even a past to unite us."

* * *

Shafi referred to the various *mujahideen* groups. Their numbers and tactics had exploded since the riot. In order to sever military communication, they cut power lines and blew up electricity sources. Of course, the new tactics also affected civilians. To the *mujahideen*, these were natural casualties for their cause to reclaim freedom. To us, it was just another day in our bell jar.

After the first couple of blackouts, when we were caught off guard without food or light to study, we quickly learned to take advantage of the times we did have power. I studied for exams and finished assignments weeks in advance. Mother prepared meals, ironed clothes, and spent any free time she might have doing other chores. She rested little during those days.

"Mohammad," she said to me one evening as I came in late, "did you get dinner?"

"Yes, Mother," I lied.

"Oh, good," she said. She hunched over and rested her forearms on her legs as her gnarled fingers peeled potatoes. It was cool outside, but her brow was covered in sweat.

"Mother, let me finish that," I said, walking over to her and reaching for the knife.

"No, you have enough to do," she said. "How is school going anyway?"

"It's going well," I said. This was not a lie. Technically, I was doing well.

"Your father is very proud of you, you know," she said.

"Hmm," I said. "I doubt he has much time to be proud."

"I guess not," she said, smiling as I caught her in a lie. "But he hasn't complained about you in a while."

"Well, then, he's busier than I thought," I said. Her face softened in a grin. "Come on, Mother, let me help you."

She looked up and looked around. No one was there.

"Okay," she said, handing me the knife.

* * *

In addition to causing blackouts, the *mujahideen* blew up bridges and the main roads leading in and out of villages and cities, leaving many people stranded, which made them easy prey for highway robbers. Highwaymen fought both sides. They didn't care whom they looted, raped, or kidnapped. All that mattered was that they got what they wanted.

People fought in another way. They joined the other side, the Communist government. In doing so, they gained the security that came from siding with power, but they lost the trust of their neighbors. One of my brothers would eventually pay the ultimate price by joining the other side. The rest of us chose smaller battles to fight.

* * *

I knew the government's influence had reached our university when our testing system changed. All of our tests were written in little red notebooks, which, at the end of each exam, we turned in to our professors. Rules and new ways of doing things had become more important than knowledge.

"What is this?" Dr. Monsoor asked. I had handed him my notebook.

"My infectious disease exam," I replied.

"Why is the cover green?" he asked, looking behind me to my friends. "You and you," he said, pointing out Yahya and our colleague, Shar Hashir. "What is this? A joke?"

"That's not a joke," I said. "That's my notebook. I covered it."

"I won't accept it," he said, starting to hand them back to us.

"All we did was put a cover on our notebooks," I said. "You actually have a problem with that?"

"Yes, Mr. Alikhail, I do," he said, looking me squarely in the eyes. "These books are supposed to be red."

My face grew hot from pure anger, not fear.

"But we only had green paper," Yahya said.

"That won't do," he said. "It's government policy."

"Oh my God!" Shar exclaimed, riveting the attention of everyone in the room. "Government policy? Whose government dictates notebook color? You're going to tell me that a notebook's color is more important than the work I put into this class? The work I put into learning how to save lives—Afghan lives?"

Everyone stared at Associate Dean Monsoor. He swallowed.

With glaring eyes, he said, hardly moving his lips, "It will do for now, Mr. Hashir, but make sure you do not alter the notebooks again."

The battle was over. Looking back, it seems insignificant. At the time, it gave us power. We left the room taller than we had entered. Victory was written on our faces. We had won.

* * *

Morad was just one of many professors who left the university. One by one, some of our brightest minds followed. The option to flee Afghanistan as a refugee had a high cost that wasn't entirely monetary.

Those who chose to leave sold their jewelry, land, and homes. They sold everything they owned to escape. They packed a few things. They maybe took some pictures and a change of clothes. Then they handed their money to a smuggler, who would lead them down one of the treacherous paths out of their homeland to India, Pakistan, or Iran.

The majority of the paths out of Afghanistan sliced through solid rock and ran along steep cliffs. Those who attempted the paths found little food or water on the way to neighboring countries. The travelers who chose to leave often found that adrenaline was no match for days of hunger, dehydration, and fatigue. I heard stories about people slipping and falling to their deaths.

There were other risks, including fellow Afghans. The very smugglers paid to lead people out of the country looted their own clients. After ripping them off with high fees, they lured them on the trail, took what little money they had saved for the trip, and beat them or killed them. Groups of bandits raped others. Government airplanes bombarded some.

Everyone knew of the dangers. Still, the first wave of refugees, many educated, risked it all to leave the country in search of a life with liberties. Instead, they found they had traded one hell for another.

The stories that flowed from the mountain passages out of Afghanistan were so unbelievable that I often wondered if they were rumored propaganda that the government designed to discourage us from leaving.

Those who stayed in Afghanistan didn't need discouragement. For the most part, poverty bound us there. We were poor and powerless, a potent pair.

Over the next year, captivity fueled fighters of all types. Escalations grew more intense as, one by one, we sought a sense of control and a feeling that we could maybe take charge of our own destinies. Increasingly, I found my power on the soccer field.

* * *

Games invigorated me. I walked on air for the rest of the evening. Even Father noticed.

"Mohammad, I know what's gotten into you," he said one evening after a game. "Come with me."

I followed him outside, where his long, slender fingers lit a cigarette. His fingers seemed thinner, if that was possible. And his face had certainly changed. I noticed the dark gray shadows that usually fell under his eyes by the end of day were now there at the beginning of the day. They seemed a permanent feature now. His eyes themselves were sitting a bit lower on his face tonight as he stared into the distance.

"You have something to tell me," he said.

Right there, in my second year of medical school, I finally revealed to him that I played soccer for the university team. He was not impressed. But, with everything else happening in the country, he wasn't irate either.

"Well, then, you've been keeping this from me for all these years," he said, inhaling a deep breath of smoke and staring again into the distance.

I looked in that direction, but there was just blackness.

"Yes," I said finally. I laid to rest the secret I had carried since boyhood. "And I'm really—" I was going to apologize, but he cut me off.

"I guess you're not as dumb as I thought," he said.

I looked up. He was looking intently at me. For a moment, his face seemed lighter. His eyes seemed to brighten with new animation, but then Father returned to serious, deep contemplation.

The secret to which I had clung all those years breathed new life into my game as soon as I let it go. I was free. This freedom reenergized my goal to make the national team.

For the first time in my life, I received real professional training. The university team trained and practiced for two hours every other day, fine-tuning our bodies and skills. And it showed. We rarely lost a game. At one time, nine of our eleven players were on the national team. I hoped to join them. It was a small goal that I could work toward, no matter what else was going on.

Still, our team wasn't perfect. While we could find unity between the lines that marked the perimeter of the field, off the field, our ideologies stepped in between us.

* * *

"Yahya," I called as I stuffed the remaining bites of banana in my mouth. "Wait up."

I threw the peel into the trash can and gulped down a carton of milk. With that, I had eaten dinner. The free snacks were just one of the benefits of being on the university team. When I ate with the team, I didn't need to eat at home, which gave Mother one less mouth to feed.

"Did you hear what Satar said?" I asked. Yahya and our teammate, Tameer, walked toward their lockers.

"I can't stand him," said Tameer.

"Come on, guys," Yahya said. "Let's just get out of here."

"How can he say that Afghanistan has never been better? That we've never had better leadership?" I asked.

"The guy is an idiot," Tameer said. "A walking, talking bag of muscles with no brain. Seriously, don't pay attention to the words of an ape."

We turned a corner and saw Satar with two of his Communist buddies flanking him. His lips curled into a sneer as we walked by. He pointed at Tameer.

"Do you think they heard us?" asked Yahya.

"Who cares?" asked Tameer. He turned around and smiled at Satar.

The muscled ape pointed a finger at Tameer and whispered, "I'll get you."

We laughed it off and left. Nothing could kill our spirits that day. We had just played well in one of the most important tournaments of our careers.

At least for me, it was one of the most important.

Chapter Ten:
The Rewards of Patriotism

Yahya and I walked to our neighborhood, where we noticed an unfamiliar silhouette. A new guard stood duty that night. He stood still as a statue until we approached his corner post. All of a sudden, with one step, he stood in front of us and blocked our path, almost causing us to bump into his broad chest.

"Just where are you two going?" he asked, sneering.

"Home," I said. With my tone of voice, I was trying to inform him that it was absolutely none of his business. It wasn't even curfew.

"Yeah?" he asked. He lifted his club and placed it into the palm of his open hand. "Where are you coming from?"

"The soccer tournament," Yahya said. He opened his bag and showed the guard his uniform. "We just finished playing."

The guard stepped back. We had definitely surprised him. I detected a hint of admiration as the furrows in his eyes and forehead softened. He tried not to look impressed.

"Okay, then. Go on," he said as he stepped aside.

"Thank you," said Yahya.

"Sorry," he said to our backs as we started to walk away.

"What are you thanking him for?" I asked.

"Not giving us any grief," he said. "Soccer can't protect us from everybody."

"It's gotten us this far," I said.

We turned the corner and arrived at Yahya's house.

"Good luck," he said to me.

"Thanks," I said. "You, too."

I walked the rest of the way to my house, opened the door, and, as usual, found my brothers and cousins home. Abdul Mateen, Nadir, and Obaidullah were listening to the radio. They constituted a nucleus of focus in the midst of chaotic play. Obviously, our father wasn't home yet.

"Hi, Mohammad," one young cousin said as he led a swarm of buzzing children by me.

He was out of the room before I could respond. I stood for a second as ten children screamed and chased each other around. One was carrying that day's designated object of desire, an old piece of rope. At least two others were pretending to possess it. The rest of the children had to figure out who had the rope and claim it for themselves.

I walked across the room to the others and joined them, sitting on the floor.

"How'd it go?" Nadir asked.

"How'd you do?" Obaidullah asked.

"I did all right," I said.

"Oh, come on. You did better than that," Obaidullah said. "Give us details."

"Honestly, buddy, I made a lot of others look good. I doubt anyone noticed me, so please don't get your hopes up," I said, trying not to get my own hopes up.

"Well, you made it," my adoring brother said. "I just know you did."

I smiled at him. Although Obaidullah was my half-brother and our mothers' arguments never ceased, we were very close. One day, when we were younger, I turned around to wave good-bye to him on my way to school. He smiled as he walked and pushed a hoop along the ground with a stick. Out of nowhere, one of our neighbor's children jumped in front of him, grabbed the hoop from his hands, and left him crying in the dirt. I couldn't do much for him right then because I had to go to school.

I spent the rest of the day holding back tears as I thought about two tragedies. A young boy had something taken away that brought him so much joy. Another child was so desperate that he stole such a simple toy. I thought, if nothing else, they are children of the same country and should have been able to share. But children don't take pride in their nation at such a young age. Lessons of patriotism are learned later in life.

"You played well, didn't you?" he asked again.

"We'll see," I said.

At that point, disappointing Obaidullah was more worrisome to me than whether or not I had made the national team.

"Shh! They just started," said Abdul Mateen.

He fixed his eyes to a spot on the floor and listened. A radio announcer's voice scratched its way through the air and into our impatient ears. He recapped the highlights of the game in which I had just played.

Snapshots flashed before me. I watched as Satar saved the ball from going out of bounds near our opponent's goal. With one sharp kick, he cut the ball to Tameer. Tameer caught the ball between his feet and carried it toward the goal. He faked a pass and knocked in the ball to score our first point. Tameer and Satar slapped hands in allegiance as they ran by each other.

I shook my head at how easy it was for them to feel their brotherhood on the field and how difficult that was off the field.

The announcer moved on from the game to the big news that we and thousands like us around the country waited to receive. We wanted to know the names of the soccer players selected for the Afghanistan national team.

One by one, the names of friends, teammates, and opponents I had known since I started playing soccer in high school, came over the airwaves. In the middle of the list, the swarm of children buzzed in the room once more.

"Quiet!" Obaidullah shouted at them.

They froze. Instantly, they realized what was happening. The older ones joined us. The younger ones pouted briefly before wandering off in search of something else to play.

What happened next changed my life. The room erupted in jubilation even before my mind had a chance to attach meaning to the words, "Mohammad Alikhail." My mind shifted from doubt to disbelief when I realized that I was Mohammad Alikhail. I rose slowly, as if I was in slumber, to join everyone who had already shot to their feet. They were all shouting and jumping into the air.

"What is going on in here?" Mother demanded when she entered the room.

"He did it!" Obaidullah shouted.

"Did what?" she asked. "Who? Who did what?"

"Made the national team! Mohammad!" he said. "He's going to play soccer for Afghanistan!"

"Is that true?" she asked me.

"Yes!" I said. "I did it!"

* * *

After that, soccer became my study. Medical school became my hobby. I practiced two days a week with the university team and two days with the national team. It was easy to devote a lot of time to practices and games. By that time, I had given up working hard to stay at the top of my class.

Not long after the shift in power, I noticed that, no matter how deeply I understood science and medicine, I couldn't perform better than my Communist classmates. Many didn't even have the same level of knowledge as me. Rather than spend hours reading and studying, I relied further on my ability to grasp a lot of information in a little bit of time. Before exams, I met with Yahya at *Chai Khana*, where he would fill me in on notes from classes I had missed. I went from studying for perfection to studying to pass.

In addition to time for soccer, the time I didn't spend studying freed up time to write and distribute *Shabnama*. One afternoon, that work came to a screeching halt.

I was scheduled to meet with Tashir and Shafi in the early afternoon to pick up the *Shabnama* prints. I borrowed a bicycle from a friend and left to meet Shafi at one thirty. As soon as I approached his street, I noticed the telltale signs of danger, a group of soldiers. I kept my head down and pedaled up to the small crowd that had gathered around his house.

"What's going on?" I asked a man who I recognized as Shafi's neighbor.

"They took him," he said in disbelief.

My heart sank. I knew without asking, but I asked anyway.

"Who?"

"Shafi," he replied.

"What? Why?" I asked.

Shrugging, he said, "I don't know."

I knew. Shafi was a very outspoken person. Most people had the common sense to keep their antigovernment sentiments to themselves. Not Shafi.

Like me, he was small in size, but he was large in opinion and even larger in courage. His words flew like arrows. Nothing was going to stop him from shooting them from his lips. In his mind, he was fighting for his country. He wasn't afraid to stand up in front of the class and voice his sentiments, write them in the form of essays, or even write them on the blackboard for everyone to read. He even cloaked his words in poetry and read them aloud at local readings and coffee shops. I had been with him on many of those occasions. I knew others had seen us together. They knew we were friends.

"What if they are on their way to my house at this moment?" I thought.

The words pierced the heart of my consciousness and knocked new life into me. I suddenly had the energy and impetus to get on the bike and ride. I turned my bicycle around and headed straight to Yahya's house. I had to warn him. I pedaled as fast as I could, checking all around for police cars and listening for the sound of sirens. As I rode up to his house, I saw that the area was clear of police. I hopped off the bicycle, laid it on the ground, and ran to the door.

"Yahya!" I managed between breaths. "I need to speak to him. Is he here?"

My greeter didn't have to ask questions. He knew from the look on my face.

And so did my friend when he saw my eyes at the door.

"Mohammad, what's wrong?" he asked, drawing closer to me in just a few quick strides.

"They got Shafi," I said in a low whisper.

"Shafi? When?" Yahya asked.

"Today. Just now. The police were at his house when I got there."

I hardly got the last word out when I started to cry. Yahya looked as if my words had slapped him across the face. He was lost, searching to make sense of the flood of thoughts that threatened to drown him.

"We have to leave. Now. They may come after all of us," he warned. "All of us. Did you see Tashir?"

"No," I said.

"Hopefully, he turned around in time," he said.

"If he was there at all," I said. "Maybe he knew about the raid."

"How could he have known?" Yahya asked.

"Never mind," I said.

We decided to hide out for a while. Yahya went to his sister's house while I sought refuge at my aunt's place. After twenty-four hours passed, our families notified us that no one had been by to look for us, so we decided it was safe to return home.

Later, we learned that a soldier traced a paper that was somehow related to *Shabnama* to Shafi. That single piece of paper was enough to convict and throw Shafi into *Pol-e-Charkhi*. His crime was patriotism.

* * *

Shafi's imprisonment made real all the stories we had heard about the government locking up people for little or no crime. More and more, we heard stories of teenagers, some thirteen or fourteen years old, opting to enlist in the army at the threat of being tossed into *Pol-e-Charkhi*.

As the futures of young men grew dimmer, Father thought more about his younger sons, especially Obaidullah, who was nineteen years old, which was the prime recruiting age. Father didn't want to see Obaidullah fight, by choice or force, for the *mujahideen*, because of the danger entailed. At the same time, he didn't want soldiers to come to our home and force his son to enlist in the army, risking his life for little reward. The choice, to Father, was clear. Obaidullah's best chance to survive and secure an income for the family was to go to officer training school.

* * *

"I'm so sorry," I said to Obaidullah after I heard the news one day.

"Sorry about what?" he asked.

"That you have to leave home to join the army," I said.

"It's really for the best," he said. "I'll probably end up fighting for one side or the other before this is all over."

"Yeah, but fight for the Communist government?" I asked rhetorically.

"It's easy to assume that fighting with the *mujahideen* is the better choice, but both sides are killing their own brothers, so they're both wrong. If I join the side that'll let me become an officer, then there's at least a chance I'll have a job that won't require me to pull a trigger. Once I'm in the army, maybe I can make a difference."

I sighed. He was being too optimistic.

"Look, buddy," I said, "what kind of difference are you going to make? There's got to be another choice to consider."

"There isn't," he said. He straightened up and looked me in the eye. "There's no money to send me to school, so that's not an option for me. This is our only choice, my only choice. Besides, who are you to tell me that I can't do something? You've always dreamed big, and I've always supported and believed in you. You chose to serve our people in medicine. I am choosing to serve them in war. If I do well enough and climb high enough, I just might be able to make a difference. I certainly will help bring in money. What difference have you made? How much money are you bringing in?"

He had done it. He had asked the question that I hadn't dared to ask, especially not myself. What difference does school make?

I pondered the question a lot over the next couple of days.

"What does medicine mean to me?" I asked myself repeatedly.

"It's my passion," I answered.

"But so what? Why should you be allowed to follow your passion and not your brother? Not Shafi?" I countered.

"I don't know," I replied.

"But to what end? What difference does it make? Is it helping to pay the bills? Bring peace?" I questioned myself.

"No," I answered.

"Do you enjoy medical school?" I asked.

"No," I replied.

"Will you ever be able to practice medicine or earn money for your family?' I asked.

"I don't know," I answered.

"Then what's the point? Why work now for something that might not ever come?' I finally asked.

"Because I can," I replied. "The others—Shafi, Obaidullah, and thousands more—can't. But I can."

* * *

It would have been easy to assume that Shafi was dead and forget about him. Many people who were sent to *Pol-e-Charkhi* never returned home. But we, his friends and family, weren't going to give up until we knew for sure.

The desolate fortress sat just fifteen to twenty miles east of Kabul's center. Its stone walls, which were erected years before but not called into service until Karmal came to power, often held many more prisoners than the five thousand they were designed to hold.

Once in *Pol-e-Charkhi*, prisoners had almost no communication with their family members. The only way to learn the fate of one's friends and relatives was to visit on the weekends.

The jail sat in an area of the desert that fed and grew beastly winds, which blew the freezing air and snow common during winter sideways. It shot scorching sand like pellets during the summer. Despite this, crowds of people came anyway, sometimes waiting for hours for a glimpse of hope. Even as early as six o'clock in the morning, up to thousands of people massed by the prison doors.

The soldiers were extremely cruel and inhumane. They had little patience. They pushed and hit anybody, including very old people and young children who approached the prison doors.

My friend Akbar drove a taxi for a living. Every other Friday, Akbar carried a group of Shafi's friends and family to the prison. We left sometimes as early as five o'clock in the morning to ensure we would make our way through the sea of shoulders and shoves to the gates of the prison, where we hoped to find word from Shafi.

"Out of my way!" Shafi's mother said.

Her insistence always took me by surprise as we worked our way through the crowd. Until our first trip, I had always thought of her as quiet and meek. When it came to her children, I learned that she was a lion. Her hands gripped a brown package tied with white string. I followed her.

"I've got to get to my son," she yelled as she worked her way through a group of women.

"That's why we're all here, woman. Back off," someone responded.

She didn't care about the other mothers, fathers, sisters, and brothers who longed to see their loved ones. She only cared about Shafi. She made her way to the soldier on guard.

The soldiers arrived in groups from the various floors of the cellblocks in which they worked. The people outside played a matching game as they pushed through the crowd, searching for the soldier who guarded their family member's area. Many brought messages and care packages, hoping they'd be delivered to their loved ones. The lucky ones in the crowd received responses as the soldiers returned with a small piece of paper, a scribbled note from the prisoner.

"Back again," the soldier said.

"This is for Shafi," she said, handing him the package and a small envelope of money. "How is he?"

"He's still alive," he joked.

Her glare told him he wasn't very funny.

"Fine," he said. "Learn to take a joke. Here." The soldier reached into his pocket. "He sent you this note."

Shafi's mother laughed as she took it. She turned around to fight the sea that pushed against us. But the soldiers sometimes returned without a note.

When they returned empty-handed, many soldiers floundered around and told the family members that the prisoner they were looking for was probably transferred to another jail or they couldn't find him. The visitors knew what that meant. Many mothers found out they had lost their sons this way. Their cries and screams were heavy to hear. Some of the women were so overcome with emotion that they fell to the ground and rolled in tears through the mud and dust.

Luckily, week after week, month after month, and year after year, we kept getting notes from Shafi, telling us that he was well and receiving the packages of food and clothes that his mother and sister were bringing. One day, those notes came to an end.

* * *

I sat across from the friend I hadn't seen in three years and four months. After finally being released from prison, Shafi had gained a bit of weight. His hairline had started to recede. But he was calmer and quieter. Perhaps he had less to say or he had grown a little more mature.

"Stop it, Mohammad," he said. "Stop apologizing. Stop feeling sorry for me."

"It's just not fair," I said. "Someone should pay."

"It doesn't matter how it happened," he said. "It happened to me and a lot of others who didn't deserve it. It wasn't all that bad anyway. I was imprisoned with a lot of really smart people. We did a lot of talking." He paused. "I learned some things."

He stared at me. I let silence ask the question for me.

"Like what?" I wondered.

"I made my stand, and I won my battle," said Shafi. "I am ready to leave and continue my fight elsewhere. If I stay, they will extinguish my mind and everything it holds. They'll replace it with new minds, void of the culture and heritage I hold. I need to leave and preserve everything I know about the Afghanistan I love."

I couldn't believe it. Shafi wanted to leave the country he cherished so deeply. I didn't know what to say. Then it came to me.

"Maybe I can help you," I said.

I proceeded to tell him of a man I knew, a smuggler, who could lead him through the mountains, out of the country, and across the border to Pakistan.

"Your sister can sponsor you to the United States," I said. "If you didn't have her, you'd be stuck in Pakistan. Frankly, from what I've heard, you might as well stay here."

The more I said in order to convince him of the plan's infallibility, the more I started longing for the same opportunity. But two things stopped me from pursuing my own escape. First, I was almost finished with medical school. Second, I didn't have anyone to help me get from Pakistan or any other neighboring country to a land of opportunity. Opportunity was key to me. I needed to be able to do something with my medical education. I would rather stay and work in Saikanda for nothing than leave Afghanistan and not find medical work at all.

* * *

My half-brother finished military training and joined a post in northern Afghanistan, where the *mujahideen* attacked his group. They captured the entire military post and took the soldiers across the nearby border to Pakistan. There, they were trained against the government and sent back.

Only months after Obaidullah had left for his post, Father received news that he had been killed in a desert somewhere between Kabul and the border with Pakistan.

"Where is his body?" he asked.

"We aren't sure, sir," the uniformed stranger at the door told him.

"How will I bury my son?" Father asked in desperation.

"I guess you won't," he said coolly.

Father was distraught upon hearing the news because proper burial is extremely important in our culture. I'm not sure why, but my uncle took it upon himself to help. Maybe it was to make up for his role in Nasir's madness.

"Don't worry. I will find the body," he told Father.

* * *

My uncle devoted all his free time over the next three years to searching for Obaidullah's body. Even though Father hoped he would see his son alive, my uncle knew better than to hope for that. Eventually, almost unbelievably, he found the remains. He removed them from the mass grave and carried them by donkey and cart to our family cemetery in Saikanda. When he returned, he told Father that Obaidullah's body looked as if it had been freshly killed.

Father never forgave himself for sending his son to his death in the war. As a patriot, Obaidullah didn't want to divide Afghanistan. But, in the end, my brother gave his life to both causes: the government and the *mujahideen*.

Chapter Eleven:
Fighting for Breath

Ironically, like Obaidullah, the "freedom fighters" didn't always fight by choice. The same guns and training that were used in the name of "humanitarian support" and in an effort to fight the spread of communism were aimed at the hearts and heads of civilians as they were forced to fight in the cause.

The Communist regime was doing the same thing. Together, I heard of and witnessed hundreds of stories about young boys who were plucked from their neighborhood streets and placed on the front lines of the growing civil war against the *mujahideen*.

"You! Do you have identification?" an armed soldier would ask me on several occasions.

"Yes," I'd say, reaching for my university ID. The first time this happened, my heart raced. And it raced the last that it happened. I just couldn't trust that he wouldn't take it and throw it away.

"You're a student?" the soldier would say as he looked carefully at the picture on the ID card and my face.

"Yes," I'd reply

"Go on, then," he'd say.

"Thank you," I'd answer.

I'd sometimes watch as the same armed soldier would force another young man or boy into his truck and drive away, presumably to the nearest army post, where they replaced their former identity with a new one. There, another group of soldiers shaved their heads, handed them uniforms, and placed guns in their hands. Then the army scattered these untrained soldiers to various posts throughout the country. By the time the boys' parents figured out what had happened, the *mujahideen* had taken most of them hostage and forced them to fight on their side. In some scenarios, they were killed in battle.

In addition, both the army and the *mujahideen* forced civilians to support the troops with lodging and food. As soon as someone took in a person on one side, they became a target of war to the other side. Saikanda was just one of many villages caught in a tug-of-war between the two opposing forces.

* * *

"Hello, Father," I said as I approached our porch.

He didn't say a word. He didn't move or even bother to flick the inch-long stick of ash from the tip of his cigarette.

"Father? How are you?" I asked, tilting my head and watching him for a response.

Again, I got nothing. I shrugged it off. Ever since Obaidullah's death, Father occasionally retreated to the corners of his own mind, drew down a shade to keep out the world, and sat where all was still and quiet.

I opened the door of our home, eager to shake off the grey silence of the overcast sky and Father's gloomy mood.

"Mohammad," Mother said as soon as she saw me, "I need you to please go and borrow some sugar from Akram's family. Tell them we'll repay them as soon as we can."

"What's going on?" I asked, looking around.

I saw that Mother was commanding a tight ship. Everyone was busy cleaning and moving things around. Even my stepmother was pitching in and following Mother's orders without hesitation.

"I'll fill you in later," she said. "We have a couple visitors, and I expect more by tomorrow."

Then I noticed that two of Mother's cousins from Saikanda were in the room. They smiled and said hello, but, as soon as the greeting left their lips, sadness enveloped their faces. The overcast sky was creeping under the door and entering right into our home.

"Mother, what is going on?" I asked.

"There's been an attack in Saikanda," she said. "It's bad. Please, go and get the sugar."

"An attack? Where?" I asked.

"The village," Mother said.

"The whole village?" The overcast sky was seeping directly into the pit of my stomach. "What about Anwar?" I asked. "Is he okay?"

"I don't know," Mother said. "I'm about to serve tea. Please hurry."

My imagination and I were falling from the overcast sky, grasping desperately for a branch of hope. "But what happened?" I asked.

"*Bad-bakht*, I don't know the details," Mother said. "We'll find out when we sit down for tea, but that won't happen until you return with the sugar. Now, go on and get out of here."

By the time I returned, two more relatives had shown up at our home. They also sat there, looking as impenetrable as stone.

"Have you seen Anwar?" I inquired of the newcomers. "Heard anything of him?"

"No," they said together without lifting their heads.

As old friends and distant relatives trickled in, my questions were met with no or a shrug. Some said, "I don't know."

That night, we reacquainted ourselves with people we hadn't seen in a long time. But the reunion was marred by what happened to our village. Mother learned that a bomb had struck one of her brothers and a young cousin of hers had also died in the fighting that, with the swiftness of night, transformed our village into a ghost town.

"The soldiers came and rounded up twenty women and girls," Mother's cousin, Jamal, told us. "And some of them were pregnant." He swallowed and closed his eyes. It was a vain effort to stop the tears that threatened to stake their territory and belie his tough masculinity. "Two of the soldiers rounded up all the animals—donkeys, cows, and sheep—and locked them in the house."

He stopped. The tears ventured forth into the valleys and rifts that covered the hard crust of his face.

"Then ..." His voice went up an octave and lost its fullness. "They lit a match and set the house on fire. I thought those sounds—the animals neighing, the women screaming, and the children crying—were going to kill me. It was the worst thing I had ever heard, until it stopped. The flames and smoke silenced the last of the cries. All that was left was the sound of the fire that raged. That night ..."

Sobs stole the brawny man's speech. He buried his face in the bend of his muscular arm.

"Bodies and ash littered the streets," Jamal's brother said as he picked up the story. "I saw at least a hundred dead bodies. And to think that all those innocent people were killed because a freedom fighter harbored in one of the homes shot one Soviet soldier. The family didn't want to let him stay. They begged him to leave, but he forced them to provide hospitality. Without hesitation, they turned our village into a battleground."

"A graveyard," Jamal corrected.

"What happened to everyone else?" Mother asked, inquiring after the members of the other five hundred families who lived in Saikanda. She had helped bring many of them into the world.

"They're gone," Jamal said. "Everyone left all their belongings and animals behind as they scattered to the hills, hoping to meet up with family members on the way to or in Pakistan."

Altogether, more than one hundred twenty people were killed during the fighting in our village of Saikanda. Many of the people who had survived left their families and everything they owned behind as they fled to the mountains, desperate and determined to make their way out of the country. Nearly one hundred villagers made their way to our house.

Although we were very poor, our family and friends in Saikanda remembered Father as the person to go to in times of trouble. Our home had nine rooms altogether, including the kitchen, living area, and dining area. Our family moved into one room. Other families, ranging in size from ten to fifteen people, filled each of the remaining eight rooms.

Anwar, unfortunately, was not among them. As the stories continued that night, I thought of my childhood friend. Images of Anwar's lifeless or struggling body, abandoned and alone on the side of a road, kept popping up as unwanted graffiti on the walls of my mind. I tried to erase them. I scrubbed and scrubbed. Exhausted, I put down the brush and stopped. I stepped back and took a good, hard look at one of the images. It just didn't seem real. You can call it denial, but I decided my friend must have made it to the mountains. I wish he had just come to our house, but he knew the mountains well. He would have felt safer navigating the land than living in the city.

"He'll make it," I said to myself. "I just know he will."

At some point during the evening, Father came in from the porch to listen to the tales from Saikanda. After our guests finished adding details to the horror story, Father rose and left the room. I didn't turn my head to watch him, but I heard the slow pace of his steps. I heard the sound of the door behind him, creaking and snapping. Soon after, the scent of a cigarette wafted through the air. Outside of greetings and the usual hospitable words of a host, he hadn't said a thing all night. I was sure he was thinking of Obaidullah and wondering how his son had spent his last days with the *mujahideen*.

* * *

There were different groups of *mujahideen*. The largest of which referred to itself as the Islamic Freedom Fighters. One of its factions would later form the Taliban and take control of the country. Many of the other factions would form the Northern Alliance that worked with the United States to oust the Taliban.

The *mujahideen* received support from Western and Arab countries that had an interest in seeing Afghanistan force the Soviet Union to retreat. Often, the *mujahideen* were headquartered in Iran or Pakistan, where they would plan their attacks against the Communist regime.

They all claimed to be the representatives of the Afghan people, but, while they said that they were followers of the laws of Islam on our behalf, they fought amongst themselves for their own ambitions of gaining power and wealth. The *mujahideen* padded their pockets through an illegal weapons market along the border between Pakistan and Afghanistan, a market they had developed. They used resources that were supposed to help end the fighting to build and enjoy a comfortable lifestyle. Meanwhile, the people they claimed to help continued to suffer.

* * *

For the next few months, I would long for the home I used to know, the home I had once considered noisy and chaotic, but now regarded as a shrine of serenity. At least, in that home, I had room to breathe. Now, with one hundred thirty people under one roof, my chest tightened as soon as I reached the edges of our property. From outside our home, I heard the sounds of laughter, cries, and screams that ricocheted off the walls and threatened to topple the building.

Walking through our home to the room in which our family crowded was like taking a walk through a market. I couldn't move without bumping into someone else. At every turn, a group was bartering and arguing over food and water. Our home was a wreck. It was filthy, even filthier than a market. And it smelled. I never complained outwardly, but, inwardly, I felt as if my lungs were collapsing, along with the world around me.

Food and resources were scarce. We were six years into the conflict. The cost of goods grew on a daily basis. One day, I had stood in line for two-and-a-half hours to buy bread.

"I'll take one loaf, please," the man in front of me said to the cashier. The man handed him some rupees and took the bread.

"Finally," I thought. "It's finally my turn."

I stepped up to the counter.

"We're out," the man said, reaching up to take down his sign that said "open."

"Out?" I asked. "But I've waited for hours."

"So have all of them," he said, pointing behind me. He stepped up onto his tiptoes and yelled, "We're all out of bread. Come back tomorrow."

Because we frequently went without electricity and didn't have adequate supplies of wood and charcoal available to us, the need for kerosene exploded. Demand far outweighed supply, leaving thousands of people without a way to heat their homes in the winter and vulnerable to a frozen death.

As deaths mounted, more children who had lost their parents were left to fend for themselves and their younger siblings. Without skills on which to rely and too young to join the army, these children had to find other ways to afford food and supplies. But children are very creative. I heard crazy stories of children who dug up graves to find finger bones. Supposedly, the children then sold these macabre tokens of war for a few rupees here and there.

"Who would buy those?" I wondered.

The fact that war hurts children the most was obvious to me, but I didn't learn this from the strange stories that replaced folklore. It was from my work as a doctor-in-training.

* * *

War victims of all ages lined the halls of the hospital in which I spent most of my sixth year of medical school. I walked past hundreds of people as if they were just chairs, tables, lamps, and parts of the décor. I stepped over their legs and moved around their puddles of blood as I raced down the halls to my next appointment.

Mothers sang to and rocked their small children in their arms. They prayed for God to restore their health. Too often, their songs of comfort turned into cries of sorrow as the mothers waited for a medical system that was too sick to bring them the care they needed in time to save their children.

Even the physicians, the so-called lifesavers, felt helpless. We worked with our eyes blinded and our hands bound. Without electricity and equipment and sometimes lacking the simplest of tools, we were almost as useless and outdated as the décor. For better or worse, we made the most of the few resources we had.

Doctors and nurses took used equipment from patient to patient, exposing them to the very diseases we were trying to fight, including leprosy, polio, tuberculosis, malaria, typhoid fever, cholera, and other illnesses that were rare in more developed countries but rampant in ours.

In addition to the problems of war, Western organizations had turned off the faucet from which aid had once flowed as freely as a river. When we needed them most, the resources we had so relied on came in very slowly, drop by drop. During the war, life expectancy fell to just thirty-six years. Statistically, two-thirds of my life was over.

* * *

One night at the hospital, a mother brought in her beautiful four-year-old girl, who was having a severe asthma attack. I remember the girl's face well. Her skin was the treasured tone of tea and milk. Her eye color was somewhere between brown and emerald. She looked like a gorgeous doll. To this day, her face is etched in my mind. I'll never forget the night that I failed to stop her airway from collapsing so she could get the lifesaving breaths she desperately needed to draw.

I was working at the India-supported Indira Gandhi Hospital, one of the largest pediatric hospitals in all of Afghanistan. The little girl just needed oxygen. I searched the entire pediatric medicine intensive care unit and couldn't find a single tank of oxygen. I ran down the hall, jumping over the patients who sat waiting for help, and got over to the stairwell. I ran up two flights of stairs, taking two steps at a time, to the third floor. I raced all the way down another hall, which was also lined with patients, until I arrived at the surgery intensive care unit. My eyes scanned the area until I found what I needed.

"Hey!" a nurse yelled. "Where are you taking that? Get back here!"

"I need this!" I yelled, lifting a tank of oxygen without apologizing.

I turned around and ran out the door. I sprinted back down the hall and went down the stairs to the patient's room. I flung open the door. But she wasn't lying where I left her. She was in her mother's arms. The young woman was holding her still child. She kissed her daughter's face over and over as she looked into her lifeless eyes and stroked her hair.

"Damn it!" I said to myself.

I quieted my mind's self-directed insults and started to apologize to the girl's mother. But the words were lost. She was kneeling now, so I knelt down beside her. I hugged her and started to cry with her. For the rest of the night, I cursed my slowness and the patients who sat as obstacles in my way.

"If only I had been faster," I thought.

* * *

But my slowness wasn't the real problem. Because we had such limited resources and facilities at the hospital, we lost men, women, and children to preventable and treatable illnesses every day.

Most of the lives I saved were through knowledge of what they needed. But knowing what a patient needs isn't always the same as actually being able to get the solution to that patient. To this day, that little girl's haunting face serves to remind me that, while I now live in a country where people and hospitals often have more than they need or can possibly use, that isn't the case everywhere, for example, in Afghanistan.

* * *

"Oxygen," I said to myself. "That's it. Oxygen. That's all she needed."

I replayed the scenario over and over again in my mind as I walked home. The faces of countless others—soldiers, *mujahideen*, boys, and mothers—went through my mind. I wondered if I had seen more dead faces than alive ones in the past week.

"Certainly more agony than joy," I thought. "Had I seen any joy? Have I felt it?"

I tried to remember the last time I was happy, and I couldn't. I shook off that thought and opened the door to my home. I looked around at the loud crowd of people. I couldn't breathe. I couldn't swallow. I thought for a second that I was going to choke on my own saliva. I panicked.

* * *

"She's not dead. She's not dead. She's not dead," I think.

"Dr. Alikhail? Doctor?" the nurse asks.

The nurse's words enter my consciousness and bring me out of my thoughts.

"We're charged," she says.

"Clear," I say, pushing the shock button.

The woman's body momentarily lifts off the gurney. I look over at the man on the gurney next to her. His temperature is eighty-eight degrees, and he is still in stable condition. I return my attention to the woman in front of me.

"That's three hundred sixty joules. She's still in V-fib," I say.

"Her temperature is seventy-one degrees," reports the nurse, sighing.

I can tell she isn't very hopeful, but she responds to everything I order. It is a long shot, but we have the resources. I am not going to give up. It is one life, only one of one hundred fifty thousand who would die that day, but she matters. I look at her still face and see the lives of millions who could have been saved if the resources had been there. She means more to me than I know at the time.

"I am not going to give up," I think. "I know the plan of action, and I have the means."

* * *

No one noticed me as I stepped over the threshold of my home. My body could have collapsed, like a house of cards, right there, and nobody would have noticed. I surveyed the chaos of our home and couldn't make out why everyone was arguing.

"I've got to get out of here," I said to myself. "As soon as I'm done with medical school, I'm going to leave."

Resolute in my decision, my chest relaxed. Air returned once more to my lungs. I pushed my way through the crowd of arguing people and arrived at a corner of one room. I walked my thoughts into the calm part of my mind, where I explored one question.

"How?"

I had a plan. I just had to find the means.

Chapter Twelve:
Connections

I knew a man, a shady character named Ahmad. He was one of those guys who knew everybody. He kept his eyes and ears open, and he always looked to make just the right connections with other people. One day, he connected with me.

"You know," said the shadow to my right, "I can get you out of here."

His voice surprised me. I hadn't heard or saw him approach. Even when it was high noon, he was a shadow, dashing about without noise. I processed the words he had said in my brain, but he had appealed to my heart. I was hooked!

"Yeah?" I asked, turning to look at him.

I sought the pupils of his eyes, but I couldn't catch them. They ricocheted off our outdoor surroundings in downtown Kabul like the sun's reflection off a blue-green sea that rose and fell beneath the wind. He was busy watching the comings and goings of everyone around us. It was as if two people were inside him. One was able to carry on a conversation with me; the other sized up everyone, looking for other desperate souls.

That's how he knew it was time to approach me. I had never told him that I wanted to leave, but I didn't have to. His skill, so to speak, was the ability to size up people in a glance. By observing others' posture, eyes, and overall affect, he knew what they longed for, what they thought they needed to live, and, most importantly, what they were willing to spend.

"How much?" I asked.

"I can get you the papers you need to take you from this barren land to India," he said. "From there, you will be able to get to just about anywhere in the world you want to go."

By that time, I didn't care about where in the world I went. I just wanted to get out of Afghanistan.

"How much?" I asked.

The words came from my mouth, but my heart hung suspended between beats as it sat still, waiting for an answer.

"Five thousand rupees," he said. "For that small price, you'll get your ticket to freedom."

He did it. He offered me the pill I craved, the pill I longed to hold in my hand, place in my mouth, and let melt away my pain.

"I'll get you the money," I said.

Five thousand rupees was a lot of money, certainly a lot more than I had lying around. I knew better than to ask Father for it, but I thought that, out of respect, I would let him in on my plan to leave Afghanistan.

* * *

"Don't be silly, Mohammad," Father said. "You can't leave. How are you going to leave Afghanistan? You don't have any money. You don't have any means. You can hardly make it on your own here under my roof, let alone in a different country and completely on your own. I swear, Mohammad, that hair of yours is affecting your brain. Your thinking has gone too far this time. I want you to forget about it and erase the thought from that crazy head of yours." "I have to leave," I said. "If I leave, I can practice medicine and make a life for myself, Father. You'll see, and you'll be proud of me."

"Then what?" he asked. "Then you'll just forget about your family? What kind of son are you, Mohammad?"

He turned away and wouldn't—or couldn't—look at me.

It would have been easy to let his words hurt me, but I saw through their sting to the suffering from which they stemmed. He had already lost three sons: Nasir to insanity; Obaidullah to inhumanity; and Nadir, the first of us to leave Afghanistan, to independence. I couldn't help but think he didn't want to lose me, too, even though he didn't say it.

Nadir had only been gone for a few months. After finishing his degree in economics, he took a job in Kandahar, where he worked for the government until he was drafted into the army. He worked one year as an economist. Then the army decided to train him as a fighter. Using his savings, my brother paid a smuggler to lead him to Pakistan before the army sent him to the front lines of battle. From there, he made his way to India and eventually got to Germany.

* * *

I sent a letter to Nadir, asking him for five thousand rupees. And then I waited. In the meantime, I told Mother of my intentions to leave.

"Oh, Mohammad," she said. "I want the best for you, but ..."

She stopped and looked away from me.

"But what?" I asked. "I'm still *Bad-bakht*? I'll never be able to do it? Come on, don't you believe in me by now?"

Her slight hesitation stung my soul more than Father's actual words had.

"No, son— I mean, yes," she said. "It's not that."

She sat and tried to rub some comfort into her gnarled hands.

"I believe in you," she said. "It's just that I don't know what I would do without you."

She looked at me and sighed.

Truthfully, I didn't know what she would do without me either. I often thought that maybe I was selfish even to consider my desire to leave. Perhaps it was time I place that desire to leave squarely in the middle of a deserted street, walk away, and let it die.

"After all," I wondered to myself, "what would she do without me?"

In addition to helping her with the housework, I helped her treat some of the pain that robbed her mobility by the end of each day. I encouraged her to walk and stretch. I brought her the medications she needed. I rubbed her aching joints. It wasn't much, but she said it helped.

"I want what's best for you," she said. "I just don't want to see you leave."

"Mother, if I can get to a country that will let me work in the medical profession, I'll be able to send you more than enough money to buy what you need for the family."

"I won't be around forever," she said, "but the others will. Promise me one thing, Mohammad. If you leave Afghanistan and your dreams come true, no matter what, stay in touch with the family, especially Nasir. I worry about who will take care of him and his wife after I'm gone."

"Yes, Mother," I said. "Of course."

"Promise?" she asked.

"I promise," I replied.

"If there's one person I believe in, *Bad-bakht*, it's you. It would be very hard for me to say good-bye though," she said. "As a mother, I would be happy to see you live out your dreams. But, as your mother, I don't like that your dreams will take you away from your family. We're connected, you know. Not just by blood. But by spirit. I'm emptier without Nadir and even Obaidullah. And I'll be even emptier without you."

* * *

A week passed. I hadn't heard anything from Nadir. My mind knew it was too early for his response to come, but I was eager and hopeful. The two qualities together were intoxicating. It was like falling in love. I was a new admirer with my mind fixed on my beloved, a passage out of Afghanistan. Thoughts of my beloved burned like a small flame in the back of my mind. No matter where I was, I could be at school, soccer practice, or home, I lived in a constant state of waiting. It was starting to burn.

* * *

Fortunately, just as the flame threatened to ignite my entire mind, a distraction came my way. The national soccer team was going on an international tour. This news meant almost as much to Father as it did to me. To the first boy in his family to read and write, news of my upcoming travel gave his son prestige. Father believed a well-traveled man was undoubtedly a well-educated man. For the first time in my life, he was proud of my soccer career. He even started to brag about my skills as a soccer player to his friends.

"You should see him play," Father said to his friend after introducing us. "His feet are like magic. He's got a gift. I tell you."

"Perhaps he gets his skill from you," said the friend. "What do you say, Mohammad? Do you get your skill from your father?"

"Yes, sir," I said.

Just by anger alone, my temperature rose five degrees.

"Ha!" I thought to myself. "All Father ever inspired me to do was want to kick something really hard."

"My skill and my commitment," I said. "I really must be going now. I have practice."

I had to get out of there before I told anymore lies. I didn't want Father's friend to see right through me, and I didn't want Father to tell me later how poorly I had lied.

"Did I tell you about his travels?" I heard Father say after I said good-bye to the gentlemen.

To me, travel offered far more than prestige and Father's respect. It offered an opportunity to leave Afghanistan.

* * *

I finally heard from Nadir, who said he had finished saving all the money I needed and was ready to wire it to me. He did so. I then met with Ahmad, handed the money to him, and made arrangements to meet him in a week to pick up my paperwork. I was really ready to leave.

A week later, Ahmad didn't show up for our appointment.

"He must have forgotten," I thought to myself.

I searched for him and asked everyone if they knew what had happened to him. I finally heard the news.

"He's gone," an acquaintance told me.

"Gone?" I asked. "What do you mean? Gone?"

I wasn't sure if my friend meant he was dead or arrested. He just meant "gone."

"Ahmad is in Pakistan," he said.

The giant boot of reality had swung down from the sky and kicked me in the gut. My jaw dropped open. I became so dizzy that I was forced to steady myself on the wall next to me.

"Are you okay?" my friend asked.

"No," I said.

The ground slipped out from under my feet, and my dreams slipped through my fingers.

"What am I going to do? What am I going to do?" I asked myself again and again. "What am I going to do?"

"Nothing," Father's voice said inside my head. "You're going to stay here, just like I told you."

"I can't," I said. "I can't. I can't. I've got to try again."

"Then you'll fail again," I heard him say. "His voice annoyed me. I'm telling you that you'll kill every plan you get your hands on."

His voice aggravated me.

"No! I have to try again," I said.

* * *

As completely deflated as that incident left me, I decided to start saving all the money that I could. Eventually, after all, I would leave Afghanistan, and I would need some cash. If not, I'd roll the dice again and place my trust in the hands of yet another person who built his life on lies and deceit. Maybe the next crook would be honest. It wasn't an impossible goal. While overseas, each team member would receive seventy-five Afghan rupees every other day.

I decided that, while I was on tour, I would live on as little as I could and save the rest. In addition, my teammates and I planned to stuff our suitcases with dried fruit, jeans, and shirts. All of which we could sell abroad for additional income. Then, just before returning home, we could fill the empty suitcases with foreign toys and goods to sell at home. It wouldn't be a lot of money, but I would save every rupee that I could toward my departure from Afghanistan.

In preparation for the Asian games, which would take us to China at the end of the year, we were going to play against teams in Russia, East Germany, Czechoslovakia, and Kuwait. We practiced a lot that year, which was good because it kept me away from the mayhem at home when I wasn't required at the hospital. But even the joys of preparing for international games didn't provide a utopian haven separated from the sufferings of the war around me.

* * *

One day, as Tameer, Farid, and I walked from the field to the locker room after practice, a car raced up from behind and screeched to a halt right beside us. A man with a machine gun emerged from the car.

"Get in!" he said to Tameer.

"What do you think you're doing?" Farid asked the unfriendly stranger as he stepped in front of his teammate. "Go on! Get out of here!"

The thugs in the backseat retrieved three more guns from inside the car and aimed the dark barrels at us.

"Get in," the man said again to Tameer, "or your friends will die."

"It's okay," Tameer said, turning and smiling at us. "I'll be fine."

He stepped into the car just before it raced down the road and was out of sight. Farid and I walked to the locker room in silence, took our showers, and went home.

That was the last day anyone ever saw Tameer. We were convinced that our Communist teammate, Satar, the one who had threatened him many times before, was behind the abduction and killing. After that day, Tameer's older brother, Ahmad Shah, who also was on the team, quit and took a shortcut down Nasir's path to insanity. I also wanted to quit, but, by that time, Farid and I, along with our teammate Mukhtar, were considering defecting while on the tour. So I stayed on the team and practiced with Satar as if we were trusted brothers. All the while, I was hoping I wouldn't be the next target of his misplaced hostility.

* * *

Though I was in the last year of medical school, after that incident, I was so desperate for a chance to leave Afghanistan that I was willing to leave just a few months before earning my medical degree. Farid, Mukhtar, and I decided we would defect in Kuwait, the one country we were visiting that was not communist. We had originally planned to defect on our way to China, but, at that time, we weren't sure if we were actually going to China. The plans were off at the moment, but they had been off before. We really couldn't count on going anywhere until it was time to go.

Before we knew it, it was time to leave for Kuwait.

"Don't forget," Farid said. "This may be our only chance. We can't really be sure we'll go on the tour at the end of the year."

Security was tight. A secret service agent followed our every move. His sole purpose was to make sure that we did not defect while on tour. Every second that I wasn't on the field, the thought of escaping was on my mind. I stayed in a state of awareness so I'd be ready if the chance to leave the team arrived.

While I was there, however, I spoke with some people from Afghanistan and asked about their experiences as foreigners in Kuwait. Over and over again, I heard stories of unhappiness.

"You're better off in Afghanistan," one man said. "Trust me. You don't want to live here. At least Afghanistan is your home. Don't leave home for this place. There's no opportunity here."

"There's no opportunity in Afghanistan either," I said.

"Yeah, but you've got your family," he said. "No matter what, they've got your back. Here, they stab you in it."

I caught a glimpse of how Afghans were treated during a trip to the flea market. A young Afghan man was trying to sell a toy airplane that moved around the post to which it was attached by a string. All of a sudden, a Kuwaiti sheikh came by and yelled at him. He slapped the poor guy in the face and knocked him to the ground. We asked our translator about the situation. He told us that the sheikh felt insulted because the toy airplane was turning just above his head.

A certain first-class citizenship was assigned to the Kuwaitis. It was obvious in lines, on planes, and just about everywhere I looked. Foreigners were not equal. Not only that, there was an accepted cruelty directed toward them.

My friends and I felt we wouldn't have much of an opportunity to make a life for ourselves in Kuwait or be able to move on easily to another country, so we decided not to defect there.

* * *

After twenty days in Kuwait, we returned with our soccer team to Afghanistan, where conditions had continued to deteriorate while we were gone. By then, my medical class had shrunk from two hundred forty-seven people to just fifty people. Most everyone I knew had already left or was planning to leave the country.

I found another smuggler. He was supposed to be good and trustworthy, but he charged ten thousand rupees. I had made only one thousand rupees on my trip. I was desperate to get the rest of the money and get out of the country. I still haven't forgiven myself for what I did next.

* * *

"Mother, I've got to leave," I said. "Please, it's my last hope."

I was asking her to ask Shaw Wali, one of Father's cousins, for the money I needed to leave the country. An army officer, he lived a good life. He had more than enough money.

"What if he says no?" she asked. "How will I ever show my face around him again?"

"Please," I implored. "What if he would say yes, but we never ask him? I need to try at least. After all that you and Father have done for him, he has to say yes."

"Okay, son," she said. "I don't want to, but we'll ask."

Reluctantly, she agreed to walk with me on the thirty-mile trip to his home. We woke up early one Friday morning and we slipped out of the house into the cool outdoors. It was cloudy.

"Looks like rain," Mother said.

We walked to the city center, where we paid one rupee each for a ride on the bus. It started to rain as the bus turned on its way out of town. By the time we stepped off the bus to walk the rest of the distance to Shaw Wali's home, the rain was pouring down.

Shaw Wali was surprised to find us, soaking wet, on his doorstep. He invited us in.

"I hope you are okay," he said after serving tea. "What is going on? Is everyone well?"

Neither one of us knew what to say. Mother was red in the face.

"Yes, we are fine," she said, lifting the warm cup to her lips to take a sip of tea. She turned to me and whispered, "Son, we have to leave. I can't do this."

"Mother, you must," I said. "Please, we came all this way. Don't give up now."

"What's all this whispering about?" Shaw Wali asked.

Smiling, Mother took a deep breath and found the strength to ask him for the money.

Shaw Wali shifted in his seat. He stared at me, but he didn't say a word. We waited for an answer.

"No," he said. "I won't give you a single penny."

Mother kept her composure as she finished her tea. Then she said, "Well, it is time for us to leave. Do give the best to your family."

"I certainly will," he said. "Give my best to yours." He walked us to the door. It was still raining outside. "Have a good trip home."

To this day, I remember the look of devastation veiled behind mother's smile as she said good-bye to her cousin. I had seen it many times before, for example, when I had lied in front of her friends to ask her for money. I was a child then, so I had an excuse. Now I was an adult, causing her the same shame and embarrassment.

"Mother ..." I said as we walked from Shaw Wali's house to the bus stop.

She didn't say a thing. She stared straight ahead. Her little feet carried her body as fast as they could. We walked into the rain. I could see the tears swelling just above her tear ducts. Like waves, they swelled and fell down her cheeks.

"Mother," I said again. "I'm sorry!"

"*Bad-bakht*," she said. "Don't you talk to me right now. Don't you say a single word. You have no right. No right."

We walked in silence for miles. She finally said, "You have no idea how you have shamed me!" She suddenly stopped walking and screamed, "I used to wash that man's socks and underwear!"

She buried her head in my chest. For the first time in our lives, our roles were reversed. I was the comforter. I held her and sobbed with her.

"Your father put a roof over Shaw Wali's head when he needed to finish his education. And now, look at him. He's too proud to help his own family. He disgusts me," she said.

"Mother, I'm so sorry," I said again.

"Don't you be sorry, Mohammad. Here's what you do," she said, looking up at me and grabbing my face as if I were a ten-year-old boy again. "You get out of this country, but don't you ever act like that man. Don't ever become so proud that you won't help your own flesh and blood."

* * *

The next day, I found out that we indeed were going to China. We would leave shortly after my last day in medical school. Farid, Mukhtar, and I solidified our plans.

"No matter what," I said as I reviewed our itinerary, "we have to defect in India."

"We only have two hours," Farid said.

"That's all we need," I said. "Even if we get separated, let's make a pact that we will get away from the guards. This is our last chance."

"I'm in," Mukhtar said.

"You know I am," said Farid.

* * *

With the exception of Yahya and a couple others, no one knew that I planned on not returning from the trip to China. Everyone expected me to return for my graduation ceremony. I was on a mission that few knew about and others refused to believe.

Chapter Thirteen:
Word

Twenty-two years later, news from a refugee camp in Peshawar, Pakistan, would rock the foundation of the life I had constructed ever since I had a five-hour layover in India. Once again, it would make me feel like a foreigner in a land I had learned to call home and in the very house I had built. At the time, that layover was the opportunity I had so desperately sought.

* * *

"So," Farid said as he came up from behind me and grabbed my shoulder, "I'll be seeing you?"

His pace fell into step with mine. Together, we walked a few feet down the hallway and moved away from the plane. He seemed unusually light.

"Yeah, see you later," I said.

Just in case someone was listening to us, I added, "Uh … back here … waiting for the plane."

Farid released my stiff shoulder and picked up his pace. I looked around. Nobody was paying any attention to him. He walked up to our teammate, Sabur, and started talking to him. Sabur reached into his jacket, shuffled through a batch of papers, pulled out a passport, and handed it to Farid.

"That looked easy," I said to myself.

Nonetheless, as I approached the guardian of the passports, a ten-pound ball formed between my lungs.

"Hey, Sabur, how are you?" I asked.

"Fine, Mohammad," he replied.

"Hey, I've got some cousins in India," I said. "They don't live far from here. I was thinking I'd like to go and visit them."

I might as well have been wearing a bright orange-and-yellow, diamond-patterned shirt. At that moment, I was a juggler throwing each word I spoke into the air as if it were a ball. Anyone staring at the balls alone would claim my act was a decent show. But anyone looking at my nervous hands would see an amateur fumbling about, trying not to get entangled in his own web of clumsy maneuvers.

"No problem," the guardian said, reaching into the inside pocket of his lightweight jacket to again pull out the passports. I glanced around as Sabur searched for my name on the papers in his hand.

"Hi," I said to a teammate standing behind me.

Behind him, more people approached now. Before I knew it, there was a long line. It seemed that just about everyone on the team wanted to get out of the airport and walk around a bit before returning to the plane for the long flight to China. I was slightly relieved.

I thanked my teammate and friend, Sabur.

I lied, "See you in a few hours."

"Sure," he said.

I looked into his eyes, and he looked into mine. I feared the unlikely: that he could read my mind, that he knew, that the very details of my plans were somehow painted on my pupils.

"Does he know I won't be returning?" I wondered. "More importantly, would he tell anyone?"

I tore my eyes away from his gaze, turned, and briskly walked away.

I wanted to turn around again and see if Sabur was watching me. I wanted to see if he had hailed the police or sent a spy to follow me.

"No!" I told myself. "Do not look back, Mohammad. You'll look suspicious. Just keep walking. Nobody will think anything unusual."

My back burned as my mind imagined a crowd staring and pointing fingers. I saw the inevitable approach of a policeman, placing his firm hand on my shoulder. It took real effort to put imaginary reins on my neck to keep myself from turning around.

"I know," I thought again as a plan formed in my head. "I'll stop to tie my shoe."

I walked to the far right of the hall, bent over to straighten my shoelace, and slyly looked behind me. I didn't see anyone I knew or anyone who looked like he was trying to follow me. I stood up and shook off the heat that had accumulated on my back.

Focusing on what was directly ahead, I noticed the crowd of people around me. As I started to walk, my eyes navigated the sea of uncertainty. I was sure I was the center of everyone's attention. What if every set of eyes had the ability to see through my pants pocket and read the address I had scribbled onto a torn piece of paper just before I left my home in Kabul?

"Stop him! Stop him! Stop him!" I waited to hear from each person I passed.

I watched their eyes for condemnation. I watched their lips for the firing of the words that echoed in my mind. I watched their fingers. I was sure the persecutors-in-waiting would point in my direction, identifying me as an impostor.

"Excuse me," I said as my usual instinctive reactions to avoid collisions with others became careless. My elbow bumped another man's arm.

"Shamma kare," the tall stranger said.

I stopped.

"That was not Pashtu or Persian," I said to myself.

My eyes now delegated a share of their watchfulness to my ears, which tuned in to the crowd that parted around me as I stood stiff as a tree.

"Haa."

"Namaskar."

"Haa."

"Shamma kare."

The lead ball between my lungs sank just below my navel. Now, even my feet felt like lead. I couldn't pick them up. For a second, I thought I wouldn't be able to breathe again. My throat tried to draw in air, but the foreign words crowded in and blocked out the air. I panicked as the wings of a meadow full of butterflies swarmed into my body and flitted along my nerves. My fingers were numb. Then, my breath pushed its way between the foreign words and squeezed into my lungs at the last second. The butterflies stayed where they were.

Renewed with oxygen, my mind gathered the strength to tune out the foreign sounds around me and focused with eagle clarity on the doors ahead.

I picked up one lead foot and placed it in front of the other. Slowly, step-by-step, I walked away from the life I had known and the people I had loved. I entered into a jungle of unknowns.

With me, I carried two resources: the address of my Nassery cousins and the gift of gestures. It didn't take more than eye contact and a nod to connect with one of the many taxi drivers and let him know that I intended to get into his car and speed away from the airport as quickly as possible.

"Where would you like to go?" he asked in Hindi as I shut the door.

"Here," I said in Pashtu.

I reached into my pocket with my nervous hand and pulled out the wrinkled piece of paper. The butterflies continued to flit. My hand shook. I hoped he'd be able to understand the address. "Uh ... Green Park," I said.

"Ah," he responded, looking at the piece of paper.

He reached over to the seat next to him, picked up and lit a cigarette, and introduced me to Indian taxi rides. Suffice it to say, for the next few minutes, my worries shifted from defection to death as I held on for dear life to the mane of a lion that dashed and darted around sardine-packed cars, each of which wanted to be king of the road.

* * *

The taxi waited as the butterflies and I knocked on my cousins' door.

"Mohammad!" Naim Nassery said as he recognized me. "Come in! Welcome!"

He looked the same to me as the day he invited me to play with the *Bamica* team. By the time we stopped hugging each other, my other two cousins, Latif and Farid, and their two roommates, brothers Akbar and Askar, had joined us.

"Here, sit down," Naim said, gesturing to a faded brown chair that looked like it offered more spring than cushion.

"Well ... uh ... first, I've got to—" I started to say.

"The taxi?" Naim asked.

"Yeah," I said. "I don't have..."

"Of course you don't. I'll go down and pay the fare," Naim said.

He disappeared into the kitchen and returned seconds later. He sprinted through the door and went down the hallway. Soon, he was out of sight.

Naim's eagerness to help me calmed the butterflies as I entered the living room. At Latif's bidding, I took a seat on the springs.

"So, this is it, huh?" he asked. "Are you ready?"

"I guess so," I said. "What time is it?"

"Just after noon," Farid answered after a quick look at the clock that sat right beside me on a wooden table.

"Well, then, I've got about three hours before people start suspecting anything and sending the guards and dogs after me," I said, laughing. The others didn't join in.

"It's all taken care of," Naim said as he returned to the apartment. "Don't worry, Mohammad, we've got a plan."

"A plan?" I asked. "For what?"

"For you, my friend," he replied. "First, we've got to get you enrolled with the United Nations. Then I've arranged a place for you to stay tonight."

"What? Why?" I asked.

"It's better to be on the safe side in case someone comes to look for you," said Naim.

"No, not that," I said. "Why am I going to the United Nations office first? I need to get to the United States Embassy as soon as possible."

"Okay then," Naim said. "We'll get you there."

The group's lack of enthusiasm worried me. Still, after a cup of tea and an hour of catching up with my three cousins and their two friends, I took a taxi to the United States Embassy in New Delhi.

* * *

"I see, sir," the gentleman behind the desk said after I stated my case for asylum. "I'm sorry, but we cannot accept you as a refugee."

"What?" I asked. "But you must. Please! It's the only place where I'll be able to live out my dreams."

"I'm sure you'll find a way to make your dreams come true, sir," he replied.

"But two of my friends were accepted just months ago," I countered. "We have the exact same situation!"

"No two situations are exactly the same," the man said. "I'm sorry."

"I see," I lied.

I didn't see at all. His words made no sense to me.

"Well, thank you very much. Have a good day," I said.

I got up, turned around, and walked out of the building, empty-handed.

"This isn't how it's supposed to happen," I thought.

My cousin Daud, the oldest of my Nassery cousins, was already in Massachusetts. The others would be going over soon. I had to find a way. My chest constricted as memories of Mother and pieces of the conversation we had about my departure surfaced in my mind.

"I'll be able to send you more than enough money to buy what you need for the family."

"Promise me one thing, Mohammad. If you leave Afghanistan and your dreams come true, no matter what, stay in touch with the family, especially Nasir. I worry about who will take care of him."

I tried in vain to drown the memories and silence my empty promise and Mother's soft voice. But it was as if I were trying to sink an air-filled raft to the ocean's floor as a storm approached. The winds blew in and stirred the current below. Still, I wrestled with my memories until I was breathless and ready to slip beneath the waves to the calm that called to me. The ocean is surprisingly still just below the surface, a different world altogether. Not ready to give up, I held on to the raft and clung to the memories for dear life. The calm returned to my mind, bringing with it the rest of that conversation:

"Promise?"

"I promise."

"If there's one person I believe in, *Bad-bakht*, it's you."

My tired bones found Mother's words of encouragement a balm to their aching marrow.

"Okay, Mother, I'll do it. I'll find another way to live up to my word," I said to myself.

I shook myself out of the fog and hailed another taxi. This time, I went to the office of the United Nations. After checking my passport and the rest of my documentation, they accepted me as a refugee. The butterflies rested.

By the time I returned to my cousins' apartment, my stomach burned with hunger.

"How'd it go?" Farid asked.

"They denied me," I said.

I slumped back into the faded chair. It embraced me.

"The United States?" Farid verified.

My nod confirmed his question.

"How could they deny me? How could they accept Daud and not me?"

"We haven't quite figured out how they decide who gets accepted," Naim said. "I'm sorry."

"When are you guys going to join him?" I asked.

"We're not sure," Latif said.

"Hey, it's five o'clock," Naim said. "We better go ahead and eat. Then I can take you over to Mahmud's place."

"Five o'clock?" I asked. "Have you heard from Farid or Mukhtar?"

"No," my cousin said. "None of us have."

The others confirmed his words as they shook their heads and looked at the floor.

"Well, I hope they make it here soon," I said. "The plane should be taking off about now."

"Let's eat quickly," my cousin said.

* * *

No matter how I positioned the sheet, balled up under my head, stretched out over my body, or pulled out under my body, it didn't help. I couldn't sleep. I cursed the heat that crawled along my skin. It itched, scratched, and tingled. I tossed.

Every time I found comfort, irony's conductor flicked his wrist and cued a well-composed noise to unnerve me. I tried to block out the sounds, but their mysterious composition captured me. I held my breath with each creak and crack of the building and slam of neighbors' doors. My stomach jumped every time I heard footsteps.

I watched the light that slipped in under the door. But the feet that came occasionally didn't stop. They didn't belong to guards or lead dogs my way. Nonetheless, the faintest sounds and shadows continued to stir my worst fears and startle my mind into jumps and jitters that reverberated throughout my fatigued body.

When morning finally came, I returned to my cousin's apartment and learned Farid had also defected, but Mukhtar had not.

* * *

Sleep didn't come easily until a week later, after the soccer team spent the night in New Delhi on their return trip to Afghanistan. I spent much of that night as I did the first, woefully watching and waiting. After another uneventful evening, my nerves unwound a bit. I relaxed my limbs and jaw. How they ached as I released them from their duty. The next day, Mukhtar showed up.

"You did it," Farid said as he embraced Mukhtar.

"It was my last chance," he said.

"What happened last week?" I asked him.

"I chickened out," Mukhtar said. "I don't know. I just couldn't do it."

"You're here now," I said. "We kept our promise to each other. That's all that matters."

"Did you go to the United States Embassy?" Mukhtar asked me.

"Yeah, they turned me down," I said.

"Me, too," said Farid.

"Damn, what are we going to do?" Mukhtar asked.

"We got here together," I said, "and we're going to get out of here together. I've met a couple of Afghans who are happy here. They aren't trying to leave, but we've got to remind each other that no matter what, we'll eventually leave."

"Promise," said Farid.

"Me, too," said Mukhtar.

* * *

Eight of us—my three cousins, their two friends, myself, and my two friends—slept on the floor of a living room, which we rented from a very nice gentleman for nine hundred Indian rupees a month. He needed the money to support an ongoing court battle.

We paid for the apartment and other living expenses with the money, six hundred rupees (about thirty dollars), we received from the United Nations. It was more money than I had ever had, but it still wasn't always enough to last an entire month. So, neighbors and friends often helped us get by between paychecks.

Latif took English classes every morning. The rest of us stayed home. Farid, Mukhtar, and I appreciated the fact that my cousins immediately delegated some of their chores to us because the chores structured our days.

I made breakfast. I woke up every morning around five o'clock to get to the milk line on time. It was a long line, and there wasn't always enough milk for everyone. I carried the milk tokens in my pocket. When it was my turn, I inserted them into the machine, or the metal cow, as I jokingly thought of it, that automatically dispensed the milk into our glass jug.

"Moo," I said to the man in front of me as his milk poured.

He didn't laugh. He said, "You shouldn't joke around like that. I might spill the milk."

"Come on, buddy," I said. "Just trying to have a little fun."

"I just waited in line for thirty minutes to get this milk," he said, holding the full jug up to me. "There's nothing funny about that."

"I guess it's all perspective," I said as he walked away.

I inserted the milk tokens and said "Moo" as I chuckled to myself. Then I walked back to the apartment and made eggs. After breakfast I washed everyone's dishes so they'd be clean and ready for lunch. Latif would make lunch after he returned from English class. He usually picked up the bread and meat on his way home.

The area in which we lived was about ten miles from a Muslim area called *Nizamudin*. A big mosque was around the corner. Near it was one of the only places where we could purchase beef. Farid and Mukhtar took turns shopping for and cooking green beans, kidney beans, cauliflower, or *dahl* (an Indian dish made of woody-smelling lentils and spices) for dinner. The vegetables were more expensive than the meat.

Our routines became boring as weeks turned to months. I spent the first couple months in a state of denial. I lived from day to day, focused only on my chores. The milk line and the metal cow were the extent of my social life. I lived without any thought to my situation or future. So did the others.

"Hey, Mohammad," Farid said to me one day, "want to switch chores?"

"Not really," I said. Breakfast was all I had. I bit my lip at the thought of giving it up.

"Come on," he pleaded. "I'm getting so bored."

"Sorry, buddy," I said. "I'm too attached to the metal cow. Besides, I don't think switching chores will do much for you. We need to do something more and bigger before I go crazy."

"Let's get the guys together for a game of soccer," he suggested.

"We need more than a few games here and there," I said. "I've been thinking. Why don't we organize an Afghan team and enter that tournament that the Kenyans and Iranians organize?"

"Damn, Mohammad, you're always thinking so big," he said. "Where would we get the money for uniforms and shoes?"

"We'll ask the United Nations office," I said. "They might have some donations that can help us."

The people at the United Nations office knew my face. I visited at least once a week to ask if they had found a European or Western country that would accept me. Their answer started off as no. Then it became, "Not yet, Mohammad." Then they said, "Not yet. But, if there's anything you need in the meantime, don't hesitate to ask us."

Finally, I did.

"Uniforms?" the lady asked.

"Yes, uniforms," I repeated. "We'd like to start a soccer team."

"I think we can arrange something," she said, smiling.

"Yes!" I said. "That would be wonderful. Thank you!"

At that moment I wanted to jump across her desk and lift her into the air. But my cultural norms held me back. Instead, I shook her hand with so much vigor that she had to push her glasses back to the top of her nose.

* * *

Two weeks later, my roommates and a few of our other Afghan friends stepped onto the Davie College soccer field in matching blue-and-white shorts and shirts. We were able to practice there from five o'clock to seven o'clock, three days a week. Our friend and teammate, Zahir, studied at the college. He was good friends with the school's athletic director.

My roommates and I had to take at least two buses to get to the field. We often didn't have the money for the fare. When our pockets were empty, we'd hop on a bus anyway and ride until the fare collector came by. Then we'd pretend that we had boarded the wrong bus and get off at the next stop. This tactic sometimes required us to take three or four buses until we made it to our final destination. Even when it took ninety minutes to get to the field, the trip was worth it. For the next few hours, I'd be at home, speaking the one language I could speak with anyone, soccer.

Seven o'clock always came too soon, but we would have a warm glass of milk and a banana afterwards. We couldn't afford real milk in large quantities, but we could afford a cup three days a week. So, after each practice, we gave half a rupee to the milkman. He would then stir the milk with a wooden spoon to disturb the gray layer of mosquitoes that covered it. After they swarmed away, he'd ladle the warm treat into metal cups before the insects returned. After that, we'd stop by the fruit stand and trade a couple of rupees for a dozen bananas. When we didn't have the money, our acquaintance would give us the bananas on credit. Our practice did more than lift us out of a depressive slump. It helped us win some games.

The bumps and bruises of the games healed me. For the first time since arriving in India, I felt alive. In fact, I was on fire. The entire team was ignited. When we stepped onto the field to face our opponents, we traversed the limits of language and culture and engaged in an international debate of words spoken only through our bodies. Game after game, we came out on top until we surprised everyone and earned a spot in the championship. In the end, we didn't walk away with the trophy, but we did walk away with "moonlight."

Some of Zahir's friends played for a soccer team named "Moonlight." When they saw how well we performed in the championship, the team asked us to join them. Although we were walking into the worst team in the league, who hadn't won a game in ten years, we were eager to join. After Naim, Zahir, Mukhtar, Farid, and I started to play with them, Moonlight began to win the majority of its games.

As our reputation earned us some muscle, we started to recruit the better players from other teams. Soon, our team was an unstoppable beast, whose prowess attracted throngs of fans to the stadiums. Everyone loves to see an underdog come out on top. Our Cinderella moment came weeks later. Out of fifty-four teams in its league, Moonlight won the championship.

Shortly after that, we found ourselves traveling by train to play teams in Bombay, Kashmir, and Calcutta. I lived for the moments we stepped out onto the giant soccer fields and pumped up the volume in a stadium of roaring fans. The fans' shouts and cheers electrified me. I rode the highs like an addict, counting the days until our next game.

The most memorable trip I took with Moonlight was to a tournament in Kashmir.

"Mohammad," my teammate, Yaseen, said as he took a seat next to me on the train for our return trip, "where is your head?"

"Huh?" I asked, looking up at my friend who had once played with me on the national team of Afghanistan. "Oh, my head. That's in Afghanistan."

"Mine, too," he said.

We sat in silence for a while.

"Too bad we lost," I said, referring to our third and final game in the tournament.

I stared out the window.

"If I had just blocked that kick ..." Yaseen said. "I keep replaying the scene over and over in my head."

"There wasn't anything you could do," I said. "They just had a better game."

"Yeah," he replied. We were silent again as the train took off. Minutes later, Yaseen asked, "You know what this train reminds me of?"

"What's that?" I asked.

"The train trips we took on the national team," he said.

I took a look around and smelled the familiar smell of metal and dust. I looked at my friend and said, "Me, too."

Perhaps he had felt the touch of home on his heart as well.

"You know what else reminds me of Afghanistan?" I asked. "The people in the crowd."

"Yeah! Wasn't that great," he said.

"At one point, I looked up. I could have sworn we were back in Kabul," I said, laughing. "Especially when they announced us over the intercom."

"That was great!" he said. "I loved hearing the crowd go wild when the speaker announced we had played on the national team of Afghanistan. I halfway expected to hear our national anthem come out over speakers."

"The crowd was something else," I said. "Not only did they look like home, they cheered for us as if we were their home team."

"Yeah," he said.

"I felt Afghanistan the moment we stepped off the train in Kabul," I said. I closed my eyes and remembered how the cool, crisp air refreshed me when it hit my face. "It felt just like fall back home."

"Yeah," Yaseen said. "It really took me back."

He looked out the window. With the following words, he closed the topic so we both could retreat in our minds to the memories that had been stirred within.

"We have about a thirty-six-hour trip ahead of us. I think I'll just relax and try to get some sleep."

"Me, too," I said.

I closed my eyes, but sleep didn't come for hours.

Moonlight offered us a pseudo-trip home. News about our team went farther than we could have imagined. Team interviews with newspapers in New Delhi, the American Voice, the BBC, and other news outlets traveled back to Afghanistan. I was so honored that the reporters even cared about how a few refugees like us helped turn around a soccer team. I didn't think twice about talking to them. But I said too much.

I excitedly opened a letter from Mother. She had been writing to me every month or so to keep me up to date on the happenings in Afghanistan, especially in Saikanda. I ripped into the letter with fervor, hoping it would contain positive news about Anwar. This letter, however, had no positive news.

* * *

This is very hard to write, my son, but I feel you should know about your father. News articles mentioning your name and the details of your defection traveled back to Afghanistan and landed in the hands of government officials. Those officials sent men to our home to arrest your father. They dragged him from out of our house late last week. He returned two days later, beaten and swollen from their chains and tortures.

* * *

My heart pounded as it sank below the shallow waters in which I had been living. My back fell against the cracked wall of dust behind me. My knees failed to support me. My legs bent like straws as my rear slipped and I fell onto the hard floor. I turned my eyes to the letter and read through a wall of tears.

* * *

They tried to force information about your location out of him, but you know your father. He is as stubborn as Saikanda's mountains. He told his torturers, "I didn't send him away, so it is not my responsibility to bring him back. If you want him, then you need to go out and find him yourself."

Mohammad, know that we are proud of you, especially your father. We hope you find a way to fulfill your dreams, as you have ours.

Always,

Your mother

* * *

The dam of tears broke. Water from my eyes rushed forth. I wished I had never left Afghanistan, but it was too late. I grieved for Father's suffering, and I grieved for my solitude. I folded Mother's letter and slipped it into my shirt pocket. Standing up, I dusted off my pants and wiped away my tears. I went outside and hailed a taxi to the United Nations office.

Chapter Fourteen:
Options

Twenty minutes later, I was sitting in front of a polished desk in the United Nations office.

"Has there been any progress in scheduling interviews?" I asked.

"I'm sorry, Mohammad," the man in a suit said. "We haven't scheduled anything yet."

"But we've been here eleven months," I whined. "How much longer will we have to wait? Please," I said, starting to beg. "I'll take anything. I've just got to get to a place where I can work as a doctor."

"I understand," he said. "We'll contact you as soon as we can schedule an appointment."

"I know," I said. "I've just got to get out of here."

"I understand," he said.

"I'm not sure you do," I countered sadly. "I know you're doing your job, but I really don't think you know the weight that I carry."

I walked out of the building and put my hand to the burden that sat underneath my shirt pocket, my heart.

"Please, God," I pleaded from my heart's core. "Just get me out of here. I'll do anything."

I continued to barter with God as I walked down the busy streets. As usual, the traffic was busy and loud. Horns sounded from all around. It was hot, but my steady pace soon had me in a trance within my head, where all was quiet. As I pleaded with God, I wondered why He should even listen to me.

* * *

"It's not the outward signs that matter, Mohammad," I remembered Father saying to me one day.

He had caught me as I was returning home from medical school. It was about a month before I left for India.

"Outward signs?" I asked him.

"Prayer, fasting, and going to mosque," he explained.

"I see," I said.

"I know men who never miss a prayer," he said. He breathed in a long drag from his cigarette and let it out slowly. "I used to wish to have their devotion." He paused, as he so often did, to flick the ashes from his cigarette. "Huh. But you know what, Mohammad?"

"What, Father?" I asked.

I was hanging on to every word he spoke. They were drops of water to my dry soul that longed for closeness to the man I both feared and loved. Finally, after I had traveled abroad, he deemed me worthy of deeper conversations.

"Some of these same men who pore over an open Koran do so with closed hearts," he said, shaking his head. "It's sad really. They just don't get it."

"Get what, Father?" I asked.

"What it's all about," he said, laughing. "Look at me." He spread his arms like wings and turned around. "I used to have money, but I gave it all away. Here I stand before you and God as a poor man. And, yet, I still give." He folded his arms into his body and bent over in laughter. "I have nothing to give," he said between laughs, "yet I still find a way."

* * *

"Hey, Mohammad, how are you?" I heard a voice say.

I looked up and watched as a young man on a shiny black motorcycle slowed down. As he pulled up beside me, he drew me out of my reverie and pulled me into the world.

"Hey, Rashid," I said. "I'm fine. How are you?"

"I'm doing very well," he answered.

"Yeah, I can tell. What are you? In charge of some big company?" I asked. I couldn't help but notice his fancy clothes and watch.

He laughed and said, "No, not exactly. But close enough. Hey, would you like to hang out a bit?"

"Sure," I said.

"Hop on then," he said.

"Where are we going?" I asked.

"My place in Greater Klash," he replied.

"Greater Klash?" I asked. "Fancy."

"Oh, Mohammad," he said, positioning his foot to start his motorcycle, "you have no idea how easy it is to live this life."

He pushed down with his foot. Then we were going at full throttle to the fancy side of town.

* * *

"This is amazing," I said, looking around Rashid's apartment. His furniture looked brand-new. The only spots on the floor that didn't shine were the ones that fine carpets covered.

"How would you like to live in a place like this?" Rashid asked. "And have all the money you need?"

"I'd love to," I said.

"Do you have a job?" he questioned as he set down his helmet.

"No," I said. "I've got soccer."

"Of course," he interjected. "But that should just keep you busy in the evenings, right?"

"Right," I said.

"Well, then, why don't you work for me?" he asked. "All you have to do is help me out on the shipping end of my business."

"Really?" Pictures of cash-filled envelopes addressed to my family danced in my head. I envisioned Father's pride and relief as he received the money. "I could use some extra money."

"Couldn't we all?" he asked.

"Sure," I said. "I can help you out. I don't have any business experience. What exactly would I be doing?"

"Great," he said. "I need someone I can trust to travel to Bombay and Kashmir, pick up some packages, and hand-deliver them to me."

"Packages?" I asked.

My heart sank as I finally caught on to Rashid's business.

"Look, Mohammad," he said, "I'll be honest with you. It's heroin."

The pictures of Father's happiness that were floating in my head suddenly popped.

"Heroin?" I asked. "I should have known. Hey, buddy, I appreciate the offer, but I just can't get involved in that."

"Mohammad, you probably don't realize how much money you could make. Look around you. This could all be yours one day—and sooner than you think."

"I know," I said. "It would help a lot, but it goes against my beliefs as a physician, soccer player, and person in general."

"Suit yourself," he said. "You know how to get in touch with me if you change your mind though. Okay?"

"Okay."

* * *

Four weeks later, I took a taxi to the Australian Embassy. This time, I was confident. Just days before, Farid and Mukhtar had been accepted as refugees to Australia.

I stepped out of the taxi and approached the building. I stopped just before opening the door and prayed, "This is it, God. Let this finally be it."

I pulled open the door. My heart bounced in before I did.

Standing in front of a wooden desk, I shook my interviewer's hand and sat down. After a lengthy interview, he excused himself and said, "I'll be right back."

"Okay," I said. "I'll be right here."

I drew a deep breath and held it, but that didn't work. My heart still flitted uncontrollably somewhere outside of my body. I tried to calm down, but that didn't work. As the minutes ticked by, I shifted my weight and shuffled my feet. I watched the clock until my interviewer returned.

"Mohammad," he said, pulling out his chair and sitting down. "It looks like we cannot accept you."

"What?" I asked. "You cannot accept me?"

"That's right," he said.

"This doesn't make any sense to me," I said. "You just accepted my friends, Farid and Mukhtar. We have exactly the same situations."

"Are they trained as medical doctors?" the man asked. "We aren't accepting physicians at this time."

"What?" I asked. "Are you serious?"

"I'm afraid so," he said.

He pushed back his chair, stood up, and extended his hand to me, indicating the interview was over.

* * *

"Stop it," I said to Farid as he apologized again for leaving without me.

We let go of our embrace. He stepped into the early-morning taxi that waited for my two friends.

"It's just that we had a pact that we'd get out together," Mukhtar said.

"I know," I said, "but you've got to take the chance that comes to you. If I was in your shoes and I had a chance to leave, you know I'd take it, buddy." I punctuated the statement with a laugh.

"You'll make it, Mohammad," Mukhtar said. "I know you will."

"Yeah," I said. I bit my lip to hold back my tears as I hugged him. "I'll make it."

I watched Mukhtar get into the taxi and shut the door. Then I stood on the sidewalk and watched as the taxi disappeared into the traffic. I turned around and walked back up to the apartment.

"They're gone," I said to my cousins.

"Good for them," Naim said. "Your time will come, Mohammad."

"Yeah," I said.

* * *

"Where are you from?" the doctor asked as he examined the cut above my eye.

"Afghanistan," I said, squinting as he poked the swollen flesh around my eye.

"Afghanistan? Oh, you guys are so strong and brave!" he declared.

"How do you mean?" I asked.

"The way you are holding your own and fighting the Soviets," he said. "It takes a lot of courage to form a resistance and fight for what you believe."

I watched him as he removed a suture from its package.

"This is one nasty cut you've got here," he said. "How'd you get it?"

"Soccer," I replied.

"Ah, you are tough. You won't mind then if I don't use any anesthetic as I stitch you up?" I asked.

"Uh …" I said, trying to hide the hesitation in my voice. "No, I can handle it."

I swallowed my pain for the next five minutes, staring at the wall and trying not to think about the needle that the doctor was threading in and out of my wound. I didn't even flinch as he pulled the edges of the suture together and tied a knot.

"There," he said. "That was easy."

"Yup, easy," I said

* * *

The next day was the last Friday of the month of January 1985, so I stood in line between my cousins and roommates and waited to receive my check from the United Nations.

"Hey, what are you doing? Go to the end of the line!" one man behind us yelled to another.

I rolled my eyes at Naim. We were used to the fights, which is why we preferred to wait for our checks together. We turned our attentions ahead and tried not to draw trouble to us.

I looked around at my companions and the other Afghans waiting in the line. We were a sight, standing in line for hours to receive thirty dollars, which is all that was handed to us.

"At least I'd be working for my money," I thought to myself as Rashid's offer echoed in my head. "Besides, what will I do if I never get out of India?"

My thoughts vacillated between knowing that I was making the right decision and wondering if I was making the wrong one. The longer I waited in line, the more uncertain I became.

"What will I do if I can't get out of here?" I thought.

"I can't think like that," I said aloud.

"Think like what?" Naim asked, turning toward me.

"I've just got to get out of here," I said.

"We will, Mohammad," Naim said.

"Well, you will," I said, snapping at him. "You and your brothers know you'll be leaving. What do I know? Nothing."

"I told you that we wouldn't leave until you get out of here, and we won't," I said.

"That's what Farid and Mukhtar said, too," I replied.

"Have you heard from your brother in Germany?" he asked.

"No," I answered.

"Don't worry so much," Naim said. "He'll get you an interview."

* * *

At one time, I enjoyed receiving letters from people—my brother in Germany, Yahya in Canada, Daud and Shafi in the United States, and Mother back home. But that time had ended with Mother's last note. I started to dread their letters, and I stopped opening them immediately upon receiving them. Rather, I stared at them and wondered what bad news or, worse, tales of their good fortunes and well-wishes for my situation, waited on the other side of the seal.

I stared at one such envelope from Nadir. It looked innocent enough, but I dreaded the words that could be folded inside. After an hour of staring, I opened it.

"*Dear Mohammad,*" it read.

"So far, so good," I thought.

"*How are you doing? I am well, but I don't want to delay my news by giving you details of my life. I'm excited to tell you that I have arranged for you an interview at the German Embassy.*"

"What?" I exclaimed as I read the details. "No way! No way!"

I reread the letter to make sure I had understood it correctly. I had, but one detail disturbed me.

"*The interview will be in English, so be sure to take along a translator.*"

"Crap! Who speaks English?" I thought. "I must know someone." Then it came to me. "I'll ask Mr. Padshaw!"

* * *

I hardly knew my English-speaking neighbor, but I placed my future in his hands. I sat across the desk from my interviewer.

"What is your name?" he asked.

"Excuse me?" Mr. Padshaw asked.

"The gentleman's name, sir. What is it?" the interviewer asked again as he pointed to me.

"Oh … Uh, Mohammad Alikhail," answered Mr. Padshaw.

He looked over at me, slightly embarrassed, but smiling.

The interviewer asked another question.

"Uh …" Mr. Padshaw said. "Can you please repeat that?"

The interviewer repeated the question. This time, he used a slightly raised voice. Mr. Padshaw looked around the room and then pulled his seat closer to the desk.

"What was that you said?" Mr. Padshaw asked as he cupped his ear with his hand.

At that moment, I realized just how noisy the office was. People were chatting. Phones rang in every direction around us. Doors opened and closed. Heels clicked by in rapid succession. I looked at Mr. Padshaw's cupped ear and panicked.

Every time the interviewer had to repeat himself, he raised his voice higher and grew redder in the face. Finally, he threw his hands in the air, yelled at me in words I didn't understand but in a tone I couldn't miss, and threw us out of the building.

"I'm sorry," Mr. Padshaw said. "I didn't realize it'd be so noisy in there."

"Me neither," I said. "It's okay. Thanks for your time."

We parted ways, and I took a taxi home.

"How'd it go?" Naim asked.

"Not so well," I said.

"You're kidding," he replied.

"Will you do me a favor?" I asked as I slumped into a chair. "The next time I need a translator, remind me to find one who hears well in loud rooms."

"What?" Naim asked.

"We hardly got three questions into the interview before the guy threw us out," I said.

I put my head in my hands and expected to cry. But I didn't. I laughed. Naim joined me. We spent the next five minutes laughing until we cried.

"Mohammad," Naim said, getting control of himself, "can you get fifteen hundred dollars?"

"What? Why?" I asked.

"Abdullah is using a smuggler to get out of the country," he said. "I don't know his name, but I hear he's good. He works with a group of people who do everything from making fake IDs and passports to arranging travel to Europe and North America."

"Fifteen hundred dollars? I'll go talk to Rashid, and I'll be right back," I joked.

"Do what you have to, but I'd look into it," he said.

* * *

Once again, I turned to Nadir for money, and I watched with excitement for the mailman. He came.

"I've got a letter here for you, Mohammad," the mailman said, waving an envelope in front of me.

I reached for it.

"Not so fast," he said, tucking the envelope into his bag. "This one's going to cost you."

"But I don't have anything," I said.

"Not according to the check in that letter," he replied.

"But I don't have anything other than that!" I said.

"Find something. I'll be back," he said.

That night, my cousins and roommates loaned me all the rupees they had.

"Hmm ..." the mailman said as he looked at my offering. "That'll do."

He handed me the letter. I tore into the envelope and read:

"I hope this is enough to get you where you want to go. Good luck."

I gave the money to my friend, Abdullah, and joined a group of seven—two couples, a child, and a man named Ashraf—who would be traveling together. Then, with each day that passed, I agonized, fearing the smuggler had duped us.

Six weeks later, Abdullah brought me a Turkish passport. He told me to get ready to leave on a moment's notice. Because our group would be departing from Malaysia and going to either Germany or North America, we would not need a visa.

After a couple days, I received word that I was to go to the airport in New Delhi the next morning. I was nervous, but I had nothing to lose. The ease with which we passed security surprised me. Before I knew it, I was sitting on a plane that was headed to Madras, located in southern India.

We stayed in Madras for three days. There, we were given tickets to Malaysia. Ashraf and I were both in our twenties at the time. We got to know each other very well during our stay in Madras. I quickly learned that he was a very nervous guy. He started our journey as an occasional smoker, smoking a couple of cigarettes a day. But, by the time we were ready to leave Madras, he smoked one cigarette after another. He'd finish an entire pack in just a few hours. He was so nervous that he had a hard time paying attention to detail. On several occasions, he mistakenly went into the ladies' restroom.

After the third day in Madras, we returned to the airport for our trip to Malaysia. While in Malaysia on a fifteen-day visa, our smuggler arranged our travel to another country, but we didn't know which one. He handed us the documents at the airport.

"Mohammad," Ashraf called to me. I could feel the fear pumping through his veins. "I l-l-lost my d-d-documents."

"Come on, buddy, you just got your documents," I said. "Did you check your pockets?"

I knew Ashraf. He was so lost at this point that he couldn't see things even if they were right in front of his face.

"They aren't there! What am I going to do?" he asked.

He tried to light a cigarette, but he couldn't. His shaking fingers broke it. His entire body was stuttering. He threw the broken cigarette on the ground.

"Okay, let's retrace your steps. Where have you been?" I asked.

"The b-b-bathroom! I went to the bathroom. I'll be right back," he said.

I followed him to the bathroom. He came out five minutes later.

"I looked everywhere, but they aren't in there. Mohammad, wh-wh-what am I going to d-d-do?" he asked.

"Excuse me," a woman said. She had just emerged from the ladies' room. "Have you lost something?" She looked at him. Then she looked at some papers in her hand.

"Yes," he said.

"Here, I found these in the ladies' room," she replied.

"What?" Ashraf turned red with embarrassment. He was at a loss for words.

"Thank you," I said for him.

* * *

"Passport," the security guard said.

I looked over at Ashraf, who was shaking in overdrive. The first man in our group handed the guard his passport.

"Are you all traveling together?" the guard asked us.

"Yes," we replied.

"Let me see all of your passports," he ordered.

He shifted his weight as he studied them. He signaled for another guard to come over.

"Wait a minute! These are fake!" the second guard exclaimed.

I heard Ashraf squeak in fear behind me.

"Where are you from?" he demanded to know.

"Afghanistan," the first man in our group said.

"You are all under arrest. Follow me," he ordered.

We turned to our smuggler, but we only caught a glimpse of his back as he ran away and turned around the corner.

We followed the police to a small grey room with cinder block walls. Everybody was nervous. The ladies and child started to cry. The men paced the room. Ashraf lit a cigarette and stuttered inaudibly between puffs. I was numb to the situation. As far as I was concerned, I had been living in prison for years. What were actual walls and bars compared to years of oppression?

An hour passed. Then the door opened.

"Hello, come with me, please," a lady with a kind voice said. She was pleasantly dressed.

As we followed her, I noticed she carried our passports and all the documents with her. We followed her right onto an airplane and took the seats to which she pointed.

As the plane took off, Ashraf and I discussed if we were going to India or Afghanistan. We were hoping for India, but we were wrong. After two hours of travel on the plane, we landed in a city that I later realized was Hong Kong.

Along with everyone else, we disembarked.

We heard another new voice say, "Where are the seven Afghans?"

I raised my hand.

"Follow me," she said.

She led us to another plane. She signaled for us to sit down. Then she left us alone again.

"That was just a stop," Ashraf said. "Now we are going to Afghanistan." He started to shake all over and continued to smoke heavily. Almost crying, he told me, "Not only did we lose an entire fifteen hundred dollars to the smuggler, but we are going to end up going to jail. Worse, they are going to kill us." He continued this rant for about an hour into our flight.

After eleven hours of a sleepless night and terrifying journey, the plane started to descend. I looked out of our window. I was surprised to see that we were descending over the ocean onto a lush, green strip of land.

"Hey, buddy," I said, tapping Ashraf on the shoulder. I pointed out the window and said, "That is not the Afghanistan I remember."

He looked out the window. For the first time in a long while, I saw a smile on his face. He stood up and shouted, "This isn't Afghanistan! This isn't India!"

He erupted with laughter.

We stepped off the plane and met an Iranian who was waiting for us.

"Are you the group from Afghanistan?" he asked in Persian.

"Yes," we replied. We were eager to hear where we were.

"Congratulations," he said. "The Canadian government has accepted you as refugees."

We would later learn that we were in Vancouver. Right then, we rejoiced. Ashraf and I jumped up and down. The couples fell into each other's arms, crying with relief. We all congratulated each other. I felt as if I had just kicked in the winning goal of a national championship.

I had no idea that the Canadian border wasn't the finish line and my race to life as I had dreamed it was not over. In fact, it was just beginning.

* * *

"Don't give up on her!" I say to the team of medics who is taking the body from me and placing it in an ambulance for transfer to a larger hospital.

"We won't," the two medics said haphazardly.

I grab one of them by the arm, look in his eyes, and say, "Promise me."

"I promise," he says.

They close the doors to the ambulance and drive away to a place that is better equipped to help the patient. After a record-breaking two-and-a-half hours of CPR, I have done all that I can do.

Chapter Fifteen:
Deep Roots and a New Leaf

The first thing I noticed after stepping off the plane was the cold air. It was May 1986, but spring and trees with new buds hurrying to burst into life seemed months away. The second thing I noticed was a face that appeared to be carved of stone. It sat upon a boulder. The face was familiar, but it was also out of context for me to associate with anything. I figured that it maybe reminded me of one of the soldiers who'd guarded our block back in Kabul. I was glad when the face turned around and led us, along with three other uniformed guards, to the airport. Our group, a tangle of nerves, followed the men obediently. We feared upsetting them, but we also wanted to warm ourselves indoors.

The airport was filled with people who, typical of travelers, belonged to one of two groups. One group was so occupied with the business of their lives that the world was invisible. The other group, sitting and waiting, had nothing better to do than to stare at others. Our disheveled group of foreigners accompanied by guards practically demanded attention from onlookers.

Their stares weren't warm and welcoming. They eyed our clothes and hair, and they took in the dark circles of fatigue that marked us as victims of weary travel. They noticed that we men were unshaven and the women were unkempt. I lifted my cold fingers and put them to my face. My hair embarrassed me. I avoided my own reflection as I walked past glass and mirrors.

Our clothes were wrinkled and dirty after days of wear. Some of the older women looked with disdain at the young mother and her baby.

They wore expressions that asked, "How could that girl let her baby get so dirty?"

They must have not realized that a mother's love was not measured by the mere appearance of her child. Those women hadn't seen what I had seen, including a mother who never complained as she stayed up late each night to wash out and dry the baby's diapers; a mother who fed, walked, and rocked her baby while the rest of us slept; a mother who, while others let their fear control them, kept hers in check and locked away so her baby felt the reassurance of her smile; and a mother who risked her life in search of a better one for her young child.

Saddened by the reactions of others and the imagined thoughts I projected into their heads, I turned my gaze downward and watched my dirty shoes move upon the pristine floors.

As I followed the guards, I had a storm of questions go through my mind.

"Where are they taking us? What will happen next?"

But I kept a lid on these thoughts. I turned my thoughts to Mother and felt a kick to my stomach.

"Mother," I thought, "please know that *Bad-bakht* is okay."

I ached as I thought of my parents and my family, everyone who was waiting for me to make it this far. I grew nervous and excited as I took the walk down the terminal hallway and, hopefully, toward my dreams. I wanted to talk to Ashraf and share my excitement with him and ask him if everything was going to be okay. I swallowed my laughter as I speculated his response.

"Okay? Are you crazy? Everything's about to fall apart! They're getting ready to lock us up in prison or, worse, send us back to Afghanistan!"

Like my companions, I was timid and did not dare utter a word, fearing the slightest breath or syllable would be the wind that blew down our house of sticks. The guards stopped, untangled our group, and lined us up. I stood between Ashraf and the young woman with the baby. She wrapped her arms around him and nuzzled him into her chest. Her chin warmed the top of his head. He was an island of contentment among us as he stared and smiled at the lights and guards before him. His mother smiled, too.

"You," the largest of the guards said, pointing to me. The three other guards approached Ashraf and the couples.

I didn't need a translator to tell me that the man whose arms were thicker than my legs wanted me to follow him. I gulped as I left the presence of my companions. The guard led me down a narrow corridor to a windowless room.

The man was a boulder. I finally recognized him. He looked like Sylvester Stallone in *Rambo*. His face wore one expression of seriousness. And his laser-focused eyes didn't waver as they searched mine for a hint of deception. He stared at me until the door opened behind him and the Persian interpreter from the plane stepped inside the room. The interview began.

"What is your name?"

"Where are you from?"

"How did you meet your companions?"

"Why do you carry false identification?"

"What soccer position did you play?"

The questions kept coming. Then he repeated a few and mixed them up a bit. He shuffled them like cards. I realized he was playing a game with me. I had to carry the ball down the field, and his goal was to trip me. After one slight fumble, I would crash to the ground. The game would be over.

I painted my answers with a fine brush and wide array of colors, sure to add every detail that I could remember. My hands shook from fear that one forgotten or off-tone stroke would be enough for "the boulder" to pick me up and bounce me onto the next plane back to Afghanistan.

"Okay," he said, stopping me mid-sentence after two-and-a-half hours of questions. "That's enough."

"Enough?" I asked, regretting the question as soon as it left my lips. "Good."

I was relieved that the interview was over, and I turned my concentration to his face, searching for a clue to what he was thinking. But boulders don't give clues, not even little ones. I followed him until he instructed me to enter another room. There, I found my companions. After my interviewer closed the door and his heavy footsteps faded into silence, I compared my story with the others.

"Did you tell the truth?" Ashraf asked me.

"Yes, of course, I did," I said. "Did you?"

I was suddenly nervous again.

"What if I was the only one who told the truth?" I thought.

From that point, my thoughts spun out in two directions. In one scenario, everyone else had lied their way out of being sent back to Afghanistan. I would then make the trip home alone. In the other scenario, everyone had lied or told such different versions of the truth that, rather than sort it all out, the authorities would decide to lock us all up for good.

"Yup," Ashraf said, smashing a cigarette butt with his shoe. "I told the truth."

He stared at the floor. The mother bounced her baby as she walked. He was not as content as he had been earlier. She sang to quiet and soothe him. Finally, he fell asleep in her arms. She sat down next to her husband, who smiled at his son's sleeping face.

From that point on, we sat in silence. Each of us was deep within our own heads. The interview managed to erase any confidence I had found since landing. I worried. But the longer I sat, the more in touch with my body I became. I noticed my feet were sore and my calves ached.

"They must have been aching for days," I thought, "but I hadn't noticed."

A sharp pain traveled from my neck to my shoulder. My arms felt as if they were coated with lead. I let my face relax and felt my jaw throb just below my ears. My ears were ringing. Concrete coursed its way through my veins. A soothing fog seeped into my mind. I stopped worrying. I was too tired to worry. At that point, I was resigned. I didn't think about what was going to happen. I just wanted to sleep. I closed my eyes and felt my head fall.

* * *

Slam!

The door flew open and hit the wall. My head shot up in attention.

"Wake up," my interviewer said as he entered the room and shocked the slumber from our bodies. With the Persian man's help, he got down to business.

"Thanks to that woman and her baby, you are all free to stay," he told us.

The words fell upon disoriented ears. It took a while to sink in, but smiles slowly emerged onto our faces.

"This is for you," he said as he handed out papers. "Congratulations."

I looked at him, but he still didn't smile or show any emotion.

"You'll have to find a place to stay, of course," he said. Then he placed a hand on the doorknob. "Immediately."

He left before the translator even started to deliver his final words into meaning. After the last phrase, the Persian man congratulated us with a smile and slid out the door behind him. Those last words put a damper on our celebration.

The bonds of family and friendship that I grew up with were such that our home always was open to anyone who needed it. With a family tree as wide as mine, I had never been in need of a place to stay, not even in India. Not only was I uprooted, I had yet to be replanted. My roots were bare to the elements and vulnerable.

"What had I done?"

I started to panic.

"I am going to die alone and away from my family!" I thought.

"If others can do this, I can, too," I said to myself. "I can do this. I will get through this. I've come this far."

I repeated the affirmations over and over and over.

We didn't know anybody, and we hadn't the slightest idea how to find a place in a foreign land where people spoke a foreign tongue. Plus, our pockets were empty. Quickly, we thumbed through mental files of friends and friends of friends who had left Afghanistan and were living somewhere in Canada. I kept repeating the phrases that I needed to hear.

I knew Yahya was in Montreal. Ashraf was working out the connections he had to a cousin in Toronto. At the time, we had no concept of the forty-four hundred miles that separated Vancouver from Toronto. Only eight hundred miles sat between the borders of Afghanistan, roughly the size of Texas, at its furthest distance.

Fortunately, just at that moment, an official-looking woman and the Persian man stepped into the room.

"Hello. I have someone I'd like to introduce to you," the woman said through the translator.

A pale man with blonde hair entered the room. The woman told us the name of the heavy-set man with a round face and blue eyes and the name of the church he belonged to.

"He heard about your situation on the evening news," she said.

We greeted the stranger. He started to talk. We didn't know what he was saying, but the translator smiled.

"He says he is here to offer to you a place to stay," the Persian man said.

"All of us?" I asked.

"Yes, all of you," he replied.

I didn't know what to say. None of us did. This was the kind of hospitality I was used to offering and receiving in Afghanistan, but was unsure if I would find abroad. I looked around at my companions. Without words, we decided to go with him as a group. After accepting his offer and thanking him repeatedly, we gathered our things and eagerly followed him to his van. The translator said he would come with us to help us get settled in.

The man was subtle and quiet. He moved gracefully and only when he needed to move. And he didn't make much conversation through our translator at all except to say:

"This is a beautiful city."

"Sure is a nice night."

He never inquired about our situation or family. He didn't offer any information about himself. He just drove us through broad, busy streets. Then we traveled along smaller, darkened streets lit only by the glow of lampposts strung together by their rays, a lighted strand of pearls. Our escort stopped the van and pointed to a stairway. The narrow path of steps led to a house that belonged to friends of his. We got out of the van and waited at the door.

A woman in her late forties answered the doorbell. We entered the home and met her husband and daughter. Then she led us to a little apartment off to one side of their home. It had a bedroom, living area, bathroom, and kitchenette.

"I think the bedroom is big enough for the two couples and the baby to share," she said as our translator interpreted. "Here are some linens for you gentlemen. There's a couch for each of you."

We thanked her, and she left. Before leaving us in the apartment, the man and our translator took us out to buy groceries and pick up some warm clothes. We walked up and down the aisles of the grocery store and searched for things we were used to having, including onions, beans, cumin, turmeric, raisins, and so forth. Instead of the open baskets and bins of colorful dried and fresh food and spices that filled the air with scent, we found boxes and bags of items we had never seen before. Many had no aroma whatsoever. The store was so different from the open-air markets we were used to that, despite the man's encouragement to purchase more, we only came home with bananas, onions, oil, bread, and a few vegetables that we recognized.

It was late in the evening when we returned to the apartment. Ashraf and I set up our beds and said goodnight. I closed my eyes and expected what should have been a good night's sleep. Then I opened my eyes.

"Am I really here?" I asked myself.

I looked around. Our hostess had referred to the apartment as "humble and small," but it was filled with the grandest things I had ever seen. I was grateful for the warmth it offered, but, at the same time, the place was cool. Though beautiful, its deeply colored and textured fabrics and shelves lined with sparkling knickknacks were as welcoming to me as a museum corridor. Even as I lay in bed, I tried not to move, fearing I would mess up the sofa, the most comfortable thing I had ever slept, or attempted to sleep, on.

"Mohammad?" asked Ashraf.

"Yes?" I said.

"Are you awake?" he asked.

"Yes," I replied.

"Mind if I smoke?" he asked.

"Of course not," I replied.

After six nights of travel with Ashraf, I knew him well enough to know he was really saying, "Hey, I can't sleep. I know you can't sleep, so let's sit up and process this crazy situation we're in."

Ashraf lit a cigarette. We stayed up the entire night. We were sometimes wrapped in conversation and occasionally wrapped in silence. We talked about our journey and our shock at making it this far. We even laughed about his misadventures in the ladies' restroom and my interrogation by Rambo. The talking helped. It erased the silence. I'm not sure what my friend thought about during the quiet, but neither of us let it last too long.

"So, Mohammad," Ashraf said after two minutes of silence, "how long will it be before you get to play soccer again?"

"Not long, buddy," I said, the shift in thought relieving me. "Not long at all."

I had been thinking about my family.

* * *

Beep! Beep! Beep!

"What is that noise?" asked Ashraf. "Turn it off!"

"I think it's coming from that," I said.

I stumbled my way through the cloud of sleep that intoxicated me and went to the alarm clock. Its red lights that read "6:00" offended me.

"But I just fell asleep," I said to myself.

I pressed the buttons on top. Nothing happened. It didn't stop wailing at me until I tugged hard enough to yank its thin black lifeline from the wall.

That was just our introduction to appliances that beep and buzz. For the rest of the day, it seemed like, every time we touched or turned on something, it reprimanded us. Alarms sometimes came out of nowhere and shook us, especially Ashraf, a bit. He tiptoed through the apartment as if he was stepping through an audible minefield.

Not only was this home very different from anything we had ever seen, it came with different rules. Tidiness and quiet are strangers in multigenerational houses filled with children. We weren't aware of the unwritten rules that lie at the heart and soul of a clean home. We were snails that left trails of mess everywhere we went. We had never seen such lovely furniture and knickknacks, and we didn't know how to respect them. We had no idea that items had a decorative purpose or they had a certain place in which they belonged. Imagine our hosts' annoyance when we picked up crystal knickknacks from a shelf, looked at them, and placed them down on a table. Our hosts couldn't tolerate us any longer. The gentleman whose name I don't remember returned to us on our third morning in Canada.

"It's time for us to find some Afghan people living in Vancouver," he said. "I've done some research, and I have some numbers for us to call."

After a series of phone calls and conversations through the Persian translator, the gentleman had found places for us to stay. He had arranged for transportation later that day. That was the last time I ever saw him.

One of my only regrets about my time in Canada is that I don't remember the man's name or the name of his church. I was in such a state of shock at that time that details, not even the ones that turned out to be important, didn't stick. His form of kindness, the type without strings, affected me. I was accustomed to giving without receiving, but it was the way in which this man gave without knowing that stamped my soul. In all the time that we spent with him, he never tried to connect with us or find and define common ground upon meeting, as many people do.

He didn't mention anything about his life. He also didn't ask about our lives back home. We were new immigrants who didn't have a single point of similarity to this man. Other than our humanity, we didn't share any family, patriotic, or religious ties with him. Perhaps angels don't care much about details. Perhaps they intuit them. Either way, our one common point was enough for this man to get up after the evening news, drive to the airport, and arrange shelter for a group of stray foreigners.

* * *

Our group split up. For the first time in my life, I was alone. I was a dinghy raising sail and leaving the harbor of family and friendship. I was on my way to a home filled with neither. To my surprise, I had never heard of the names that belonged to the Afghans who were about to welcome me. My hands shook as I fiddled with my shirt in the backseat of the taxi. I was accustomed to, at the very least, knowing an Afghan's family by reputation. For the first time in my life, this wasn't the case.

When my new hosts opened the door that afternoon, I was taken aback. They were weary and slow. They let me in, showed me to my bed, and went to sleep. I was surprised they didn't offer tea or conversation, but the exhausted part of me was grateful. I fell asleep.

Later that night, I woke up bewildered as my hosts rose and started to make noise. They turned on their music and pumped their bodies with drugs. I turned down their offers. I was relieved when they left the apartment for a night of partying. They returned the next morning and stumbled their way to bed just as I was rising for the day.

That day, I came down with the flu. My vomiting and weariness trapped me between the toilet and turmoil. I spent much of the next week not knowing if it was night or day or where I was. I stayed in bed almost the entire time that I was there, and I kept the pillow over my head.

When I wasn't sleeping or confused from the illness, reality came into focus. I realized that agony's hand dangled my stomach above me. The pain of isolation from my family and the strangeness of my drugged hosts threatened to capsize my sanity. I felt little control over my situation and much preferred the flu-induced state of confusion that forced me to forget about my situation.

About a week after my arrival, one of the men came to me and said, "Hey, Mohammad, I got some news for you."

"Yeah?" I asked.

I was sure he was going to kick me out, and I wasn't quite sure if that would be the worst thing that could happen to me.

"I ran into a guy named Naquibullah," he said. "He says he knows you."

"Naquibullah?" It didn't hit me right away, but then his face came to mind. I remembered that his family lived near mine in Kabul. "Yeah, I know him."

"Well, get up and get your things together. He's on his way to come and get you."

A half hour later, I was riding in a weathered, old truck with a family friend. He took me to the apartment he shared with four of his brothers. We sat, drank tea, and talked all night long.

* * *

Naquibullah knew exactly what I needed to do. The next day, he took me to the welfare office and helped enroll me with public assistance, which gave me two hundred twenty dollars a month. Within a week, he and his brothers found a place for me to live. It was a small basement apartment that rented for one hundred sixty dollars a month, everything included, leaving sixty dollars for a month for groceries and bus fare.

The apartment was located on Woodstock Avenue in the eastern part of Vancouver. Two other rooms were in the apartment. The tenants of all three rooms shared the kitchen, living room, and bathroom.

The apartment came with a short list of rules that the owner, who lived above us, dictated. No smoking was allowed. We could not fry onions or control the heat. The first one didn't affect me at all. I found the second one rather strange. I knew of very few dishes that didn't have onion, but it was a minor inconvenience. The third one bothered me. The owner of the house turned on the heat when he wanted. The rest of the time, we froze in the basement, the coolest part of the house. Nevertheless, all in all, it was a great apartment. It was conveniently located, and it offered privacy, something I had never known.

I was twenty-five years old, and I finally learned what privacy was like. I did the things I wanted to do and when I wanted. I woke up when I wanted and ate when I wanted. Although it was a small, dirty room in a basement, I felt the warmth of peace for the first time in years. I rested.

Up until that time, I had been exhausted, emotionally and physically. I was constantly in a state of agony. The agony didn't stop completely, but I was able to reclaim my stomach and move the worry to the back of my mind. I prayed and read books and set out on my next task of learning English.

I tried to teach myself. Every morning, I went out to the common room and turned on the TV in search of a soccer game. I didn't find many, but I did find that just about any sport was entertaining enough to capture my attention. After just a few weeks, I had learned enough English to get by around town.

* * *

After getting my second check, I had enough money to write to Yahya and tell him of my arrival and call my brother in Germany. It was nice to reconnect with friends and family. My brother caught me up on what was happening with my brothers and our parents. And I caught him up on my life and my newly found dual-edged sword of privacy and loneliness.

"It gets better, you know," he said. "Have you looked for a job?"

"No, not yet," I replied.

"You've got to find a job, Mohammad," he said. "It's the most important thing."

"Well, I get some money from the government. It's helping me get by until I learn enough English," I said.

"You know enough English," he said. "You're just afraid."

"I'm not afraid," I said indignantly to my older brother.

"Trust me, I've been there," he said. "You may not start out in your field, but the longer you take to get up and build a life, the harder it will be."

He was right, and I knew it. Up until then, I was just focused on learning English and not thinking at all about the bigger picture.

"So what do you want me to tell our mother when I talk to her?" Nadir asked.

"Tell her that I'll be okay and I'm looking for a job," I replied.

Chapter Sixteen:
Nametags and Timecards

I had left Afghanistan to build a better life. Not only did I want to find a life that was easier and wealthier, I wanted one that was fulfilling and would ease my family's suffering. Like my parents and everyone else in the world, I was born with a unique set of abilities. Father's gifts helped him become the first literate man in his family. Mother's gifts identified her as one of the most compassionate women in our village. I chose to apply my gifts to soccer and medicine. The first helped save my life. I hoped the second would bring meaning to it.

I had made it to Canada and found a place to live. Now, I faced another set of problems: language, motivation, and money. A job would help me overcome all three.

* * *

"Mohammad," my neighbor said to me when she came into the common area. "You need to turn off the TV and get a job."

"I can't," I said as I watched the commercials.

"Why not?" she asked.

"My English," I said.

"You can talk to me," she replied.

"That's different," I said.

"Then go get English lessons," she directed.

"I don't have enough money," I said.

"See," she said. "You need to get out of here and go look for a job. You've been watching *Three's Company* and sports for three months now."

"They teach me," I said. "Besides, I don't know how to do anything."

"What?" she asked. "You're a doctor. If you can get a medical degree, you can deliver pizzas."

"I don't want to deliver pizzas," I said.

"And I don't want to wait tables," she replied.

She was right, but I was lazy. And I was still afraid. It seems weird when I think back to that time. I had never been too afraid of anything. I certainly didn't mind thinking big and taking risks, but that was in Afghanistan, where I knew the culture and the language.

Luckily, a job came to me.

* * *

"Hey, buddy," I said to Naquibullah. We were meeting for a game of soccer. "Where are the others?"

"They'll be along later," he said. A grin was planted on his face. "Want a job?"

"What?" I asked.

"Come with me. I want to introduce you to someone," he said.

We walked to Mac's Store, where Naquibullah introduced me to Moc Lucina, a Filipino guy who ran the convenience store. Moc offered me four dollars an hour to work the graveyard shift from eleven o'clock at night to seven o'clock in the morning. I accepted.

* * *

Like most people, I was nervous about my first day of work. By the time my shift ended, I was depressed. I had never touched a cash register before that day. Back home, we still used scales to price food. Merchants weighed customers' items, calculated the costs in their heads, and always exchanged the items for cash. Checks and credit cards were completely new concepts to me.

My cash drawer was fifty dollars short. I was afraid that I'd be fired and accused of stealing. Moc had been an accountant in the Philippines. He instantly realized that I had wrongly keyed some numbers. He pointed out my mistakes and was kind enough not to make a big deal about the money. He reassured me that I would improve.

He was right. My skills sharpened quickly, but my difficulties with English led to other problems. Sometimes, I misunderstood words.

* * *

"We don't sell pork," said the voice on the other end.

"But I was told to call you and order three hundred porks," I insisted.

We continued to argue. I hung up the phone, disappointed I had failed Moc. Reluctantly, I called him to tell him that I must have written down the wrong phone number.

"You didn't get the number wrong, Mo," he said, laughing. "You got the word wrong. We need forks. Forks!" By this time, he could hardly control the laughter. "Not porks!"

At other times, I didn't know the words.

"Where is your whipped cream, little man?" asked a very large, very tattooed customer.

"I don't know, sir," I replied.

I didn't know where it was because I didn't know what it was.

"Who the hell hired you?" he asked rhetorically.

"A friend of mine knew this other guy named Moc, and he hired me," I answered.

He scoffed at me, turned away, and proceeded up and down the aisles until he found a metal tube. He held the can in front of my eyes and said,

"This," he slammed the can down on the counter, "is whipped cream."

That was one English lesson I'll never forget.

I decided it was time to expand my vocabulary. That week, I enrolled in an English course at one of the area community colleges. The class went from eight o'clock in the morning to three o'clock in the afternoon, Mondays through Friday. I slept from four o'clock to ten o'clock and then went to work. Then I went to school the next morning. I didn't have much time to study for my class, but I caught on rather quickly. It was a nice break, compared to my job.

People did and said crazy things in the middle of the night. One guy tried to return a ninety-nine cent cigarette lighter a few days after he bought it. He said it didn't work, and he wouldn't admit that he had used all of the fuel.

"There's nothing I can do for you," I told him for the third time. "Why can't you understand that?"

"Who the heck are you?" he asked. "I understand. This is my country! Do you understand? You damn foreigner! Why don't you go back to the country you came from? All you want is our money anyway."

His reaction was pretty typical. Every time someone didn't get his or her way, it all came down to my status as a foreigner. In fact, many people appeared to believe that all of their problems would be solved if I just turned around, got on a boat, and went home.

In addition to the people who blamed my nationality on all of their problems were the people who were just plain drunk. I was shocked the first time someone mooned me.

"What's that about?" I asked Moc, who happened to be there. "Is that guy crazy or what?"

"Yeah, that," he said. "He's not crazy. He's just drunk. You better just get used to that kind of behavior."

I got used to it. Fortunately, I never had to see most of the people who pulled stunts like that for a second time. The regulars were generally pretty typical. I liked them. Mr. Miller came to the store every couple weeks to turn in empty bottles for a refund. Then he'd turn right around and spend that money on alcohol. The only time he didn't look depressed and downtrodden were the days right after he received his welfare check. Those were the only times he didn't have to "work" to keep his body buzzed on booze.

"Hey Mohamma'," he'd say as he slid a quarter my way. "This is for you. Take it, and call a taxi for me, will ya?"

"Keep your money, Mr. Miller. I'll call the cab," I'd say as I slid the quarter back across the counter while trying not to breathe any of the air that was between us. It was stale and heavy.

"Why are you spending your money like this?" I'd ask him.

Part of me knew the answer. I had known plenty of people like Mr. Miller throughout my life. They may not have turned to alcohol, but they had other ways of drowning their pain.

"Don't ya worry 'bout me," he'd say, smiling. "I'll be all right."

The cycle repeated every few weeks. He wore a smile right after getting his check, but, just a couple of days later, he rattled his way to the store with a grocery cart filled with empty bottles. Again, I'd try to talk him into doing something better with his time and money.

Mr. Ivin came in every morning with an empty coffee mug. He was an older gentleman with a lot of money and even more frugality. He owned the apartment building next to the convenience store, which was just one of many under his name. He had worked out a deal that traded parking for coffee, so he visited the store every morning. He filled up his own coffee mug and read the newspaper. He didn't buy it, but he certainly could have afforded it. He read it, refolded it, and returned it to the rack. Mr. Ivin was very rich and owned a lot of real estate, but he hardly spent a dime in the store or anywhere else.

* * *

I worked hard at the store, and Moc noticed. After three months, he promoted me to the evening shift, which started at three o'clock in the afternoon and finished at eleven o'clock at night. The hours were better, and the people weren't quite as strange. I was able to take a morning English class to accommodate the new schedule.

Most days were filled with hard work and negativity. Ninety percent of the people with whom I talked were either rude or flat-out discouraging. But there were some regular, everyday people whose small moments of encouragement were enough to get me through the day and stick with the job. There were also those who reminded me that I wanted more.

One of those people was the milkman from India.

"Mo," he'd say, "try to learn the language. You've got to pursue your medical dreams. Look at me, I'll be a milkman forever, but I don't think you'll always be a cashier."

He was right. I wasn't always a cashier. I sometimes worked odd construction jobs for Naqibullah.

One day, Naqibullah didn't have a painter for a home he was remodeling. The painter he had asked wouldn't take less than fifteen dollars an hour to do the job, so my friend asked me instead. I agreed to do the job for only five dollars an hour. He hired me on the spot. Unprepared, I improvised and did the best I could.

I didn't want to ruin my clothes, so I tore a hole in the top of a black garbage bag, tore two holes on the sides, placed it over my head and painted the house. I used more paint than a professional painter would have used, but, nonetheless, I finished the house in only a couple days of work. Another painter who was working on a house in the neighborhood came by. After seeing my work, he asked if I was a professional painter. I told him that I wasn't, but he liked my job so much that he asked if he could call me when he needed a painter. I told him that would be fine. I felt like a dog that had been petted for the first time in months.

It didn't take me long to realize that my Mac's Store nametag transformed me from a person with abilities and talents into a mere button-pusher, an inconvenient barrier between the customers and their goods. I was still the same person I had been in medical school, someone with unique potential, but no one saw that. Rather, they saw an opportunity to look down on someone and feel better about themselves, if they saw me at all.

In addition to working those jobs, Naqibullah's brother, Nisar, and I worked odd landscaping jobs. Nisar was trained as a veterinarian. He and I had a lot in common, and we were the same age. We usually had a good time working together. I used to hang flyers in area Laundromats to find the jobs, and we hauled our equipment with his truck. We also used the truck to deliver and pick up furniture for our friend, Ahmad Sear, an Afghan who worked with a local furniture store. Most of the time, he'd give the deliveries to professionals, but, if the delivery wasn't very big, he'd pay us fifty to one hundred dollars to carry the furniture. It didn't bother me to work hard on odd jobs. But it frustrated me no end to work for dishonest people.

One day, Nisar and I took a weekend job at a bakery. The owner offered to pay each of us six dollars an hour to clean the building and wash the dough from the equipment. The equipment was disgusting. By the end of the job, we were exhausted. We went to collect our paychecks when this gentleman told us that he wouldn't pay us until we cleaned the bathrooms. I was enraged, but I cleaned the bathrooms anyway because he had our money. We returned to him. I faced one of the most frustrating moments in my life when he told us that he was only going to pay the both of us forty dollars when each of us had earned more than that.

* * *

Naquibullah, his brothers, and our friends, Abdul Wahab Alawi, Aziz Ghani, and Najibullah Bakhtary, worked hard together, but we also played hard. I lived for the weekends. I got in a game of basketball or soccer when I wasn't studying English or working extra jobs.

One day, Wahab was driving a group of us in Aziz's car to northern Vancouver for a soccer game. He had just received his learner's permit, and he was very eager to drive. He was turning left at an intersection on Broad Street. He swerved into the path of an oncoming bus, which hit our car in the back and spun us around a couple times. None of us was injured, but the car was dinged up a bit where it was hit. We continued on to the game and lost. We were more upset about losing the game than the car accident.

Aziz didn't bother repairing the 1972 Toyota Crown. The car continued to fall apart. At one point, it lost the ability to go into reverse gear. Aziz finally decided to sell the car. I asked him if I could buy it. He didn't want to sell it to me because it was in such bad shape, but I convinced him otherwise. With six hundred dollars, I bought my first car. I drove without reverse gear for one month. Then I found a mechanic to install an old transmission for three hundred sixty dollars. After that, I had a fully functional car.

The car allowed me to take a job delivering pizzas. Bella Pizza was a tiny shop on the corner of Broadway and Hemlock in Vancouver. Three guys, a Greek, a Chinese, and a Canadian, owned the shop. The job paid drivers five dollars an hour plus gas expenses, 25 percent more than I had received for working at Mac's Store.

But, during my first day on the job, the car stopped running in the middle of a delivery. I turned the key in the ignition again and again, but nothing happened. So I pushed the car to the side of the road and hailed a taxi. I paid the taxi driver four dollars to help me deliver the pizza hot and on time. When I called the guys at the pizza shop to ask for a jump start, I told them what happened. The entire shop burst into laughter.

"Man, you paid four dollars in order to make five?" asked the guy who drove out to jump-start my car battery. "You're an idiot."

And here I thought I was a dedicated worker! By the time I returned to the shop, I could laugh along with the others.

The pizza job wasn't bad. When there weren't any pizzas to deliver, we prepared for future orders and cut up mushrooms, onions, green peppers, and cheese. I was willing to do just about anything there, but I'd cringed when I heard my boss say, "Hey, Mobuddy, why don't you get started on those dishes?"

"Sure thing," I'd say as I put down the knife, roll my sleeves up above my elbow, and make my way to the sink.

The sink was very big and deep. The smell of the water gagged me. I couldn't even reach the bottom without leaning into it. Dishes were sometimes packed from top to bottom. Then, like a great volcano, a mound would surface from the greasy water. It was the nastiest job there. None of us wanted to do it. As the dishes started to pile up, we prayed for deliveries, even one of the bad ones. And there were plenty of those.

One day, I arrived at a pizza delivery location in east Vancouver and knocked on the door. Nobody answered. I continued to knock. Still, there was no answer. Finally, I knocked as hard and loudly as I possibly could without ripping open my knuckles.

"Hey, you!" a drunken Hispanic neighbor yelled from my right. "Stop knocking on that door!".

I continued to knock because I didn't want the pizza to be wasted. Also, I wanted to see if I could get a tip. The Hispanic guy closed in on me and started yelling in my face.

"If you don't get out of here," he yelled through a fog of bad breath, "I'm going to kill you!"

I brushed it off as just another drunken threat. After so many of those, it was hard to take them seriously.

"Go mind your own business," I said.

The man left, and I continued knocking. But, the next thing I knew, the guy came rushing out of his house and raised a large butcher knife.

"Whoa, buddy, what are you doing?" I asked him.

"I'm not your buddy!" he yelled.

He lunged toward me and stabbed the knife into the wall behind where I was standing. I put my soccer agility and speed to use and got to the car as fast as I could, which, compared to him, was pretty fast.

It wasn't often that I felt I was in danger of losing my life, but people often looked at me with contempt. And, just like at Mac's Store, they let me know it. They yelled at me for being late or showing up with cold pizza. It was hard to deliver pizza on time in the winter or during rush hour traffic. Some grabbed the pizza and refused to pay. Others paid partially.

"That'll be eleven dollars and forty-five cents," I said as I handed one customer his pizza at nearly four o'clock in the morning.

"Here, take this," he said, holding out a jar of pennies. "That ought to be good enough."

"Sir, could you please count these?" I asked. "I don't know how much money is in that jar."

"Okay, just come inside."

As I entered his home, I smelled stale beer, which only confirmed my assumption that his red eyes weren't entirely due to a late night. I went in. He dumped the pennies on the coffee table and started to count them. He got up around one hundred and lost count.

"Damn it," he said. He shook his head, strained his eyes to focus, and started separating pennies, one by one, from the pile.

"Thirty-four, thirty-five." Then he paused. "Where was I?"

The more he started over, the more frustrated he grew. He started throwing insults at me. After some time, he realized the money wasn't going to be enough.

"Here, take it," he said. "That's all I've got."

"But that's only eight dollars. I need three dollars and fifty cents more."

As those last words came out of my mouth, I could tell he was about to lose his patience with me, so I headed for the door.

"Go. Get out of here. Damn you, you fucking Punjabi. Get out of my country!" he yelled.

"I'm not Punjabi," I retorted. "I'm from Afghanistan."

Once again, my truthful words fell upon deaf ears. To him, I was just another foreigner.

If people weren't picking on me for being a foreigner, it was for something else, including being poor, working at a dead-end job, or wearing neat clothing. None of which defined me. They just described me.

"Hey, look at this guy," one man said to his friends inside. "He's got on some fancy clothes. Who do you think you are?" he asked, turning his attention to me.

He stared at me. His face was red with anger. My face was red with anger as well. But I thanked him for paying and left.

More than once, people commented on my cleanliness. I didn't understand why that was a big deal to other people.

"Are poor people not supposed to have any dignity or self-respect?" I wondered.

On many nights, I left the deliveries in tears. But the job had perks.

One time, I delivered a pizza to a fancy-looking apartment building. I knocked on the door. A tough-looking guy opened it.

"How much?" he asked.

I told him the cost.

"Wait here," he said. "I'll be right back."

He had left the door ajar. A movement within the apartment caught my eye. I focused in that direction and saw I was staring at a mirror that allowed me to see into a bedroom. Standing before me was one of the most beautiful women I had ever seen. And she was naked. She had no idea that I could see her. I'm not sure how much time passed. It could have been seconds or minutes. The guy eventually returned to the door and handed me the money.

"Enjoy the pizza and Coke," I said.

I swallowed hard and tore my eyes away from the mirror.

* * *

The perks weren't often or great enough to keep me at that job. I stayed interested in finding new ways to make money and have fun. I never really stopped playing soccer. I played with my friends. I eventually knew enough guys to start an Afghan soccer team in Vancouver. We weren't one of the outstanding teams, but we did fairly well in the several tournaments we played each year. We practiced three to four times a week, which served me well. I stayed in shape and continued to stay out of the darker pastimes, like alcohol and drugs, that consumed so many other immigrants that I knew.

An Iranian guy on our team asked me what I was doing for a living.

"I deliver pizzas," I answered.

"Pizzas? I did that. I drive taxis now," he said. "There's a lot more money in taxis."

"Really?" I asked.

"You know, I could put in a good word for you if you like," he offered.

I figured I didn't have much to lose so I said, "I'd like that."

The following week, I went to the head office of Black Top Taxi, where my Iranian friend introduced me to his boss. I filled out an application. Things moved quickly from there. First, I had to pass a driving exam in order to get a license to drive a taxi. Then I had to pass a written exam of the streets and locations in Vancouver. The first exam was pretty easy. And the second was also easy because of my experience delivering pizzas. The real tests came when I finally got behind the wheel of my first taxi.

Once again, my job offered moments filled with happiness, frustration, and tears. My work as a taxi driver was different, but it was also the same. It was another service-oriented job that dealt with the public.

One of the most interesting things I learned during my days of driving a taxi was that rich people, in general, were surprisingly cheap; it wasn't just Mr. Ivin. On many nights, I drove fancy-looking passengers from one fine place, such as a five-star hotel, to another fine place. Ironically, they were, by far, the stingiest tippers. They usually tipped about fifty cents per ride, even for the longer ones. On the other hand, the average-looking customers were usually the most generous tippers. They tipped three to four dollars a ride, no matter how long the distance.

Some people didn't tip at all; some didn't even pay the fare. One day, I drove a gentleman from downtown Vancouver to the eastern part of the city, about ten to fifteen miles away. He asked me to wait in the taxi while he went into an apartment building to check on his girlfriend. His girlfriend wasn't there, so he came back and told me to take him back to the city. I was excited about the rare round-trip fare. After we returned to the city, he asked me to wait again while he ran into another apartment.

I realized this guy didn't intend to pay me, so I said, "Sorry, sir, but you are going to have to pay the twenty-five dollar fare first or I'll call the police."

"Oh, yeah?" he said. He reached in his jacket pocket, pulled out a knife, and pointed it at my face. "What if I put this knife in you, taxi driver? Who are you going to call then?"

"Okay," I said, "just go away."

He took off toward the building, and I called the police.

On another night, I picked up a couple of teenagers, a girl and a boy. They asked me to take them from the downtown area to northern Vancouver, which is quite a trip. I drove a little fast so I could make it there and back quickly and get another fare. The guy was very drunk. He started yelling and swearing at me.

When it came time to pay the fare, he said, "You damn foreigner, you have the nerve to come to my country and try to rip me off? I'm not paying that. You must have rigged the meter to go faster because the trip I took was not that long."

"You pay for the distance, not the time," I said.

I tried explaining to him that, just because I drove faster, it didn't mean that the distance was shorter. But he was drunk and angry, and he wasn't in the mood for mathematics. Despite his bad temper, his girlfriend seemed to be a very nice young woman. She gave me an apologetic smile and tried to calm him down. He didn't pay me, but he continued to yell at me and make inflammatory remarks. I just endured it.

I endured a lot in the taxi, even when there weren't any passengers. I honestly don't know which was worse, actually dealing with negative people or being alone in the cab. When I didn't have any passengers, I read the paper to pass the time. Sometimes, though, I just sat in the driver's seat and stared at the fine black print while my mind wandered into very deep thoughts about myself and my life. I weighed my decision to leave my home and family behind. I wondered if it was worth it.

"If I had stayed in Afghanistan, could I be working as a doctor?" I thought.

I would have been living in a war situation, but I would have been a doctor. I'd have the respect that I enjoyed in the country as a national soccer player and medical student.

I hardly had any respect in Canada. My friends respected me, but most of the people who interacted with me as a store clerk, pizza delivery person, or taxi driver treated me like a nobody. As I look back now, I wonder if the nickname "Mobuddy" was just another joke that I didn't get. I wondered if all my effort was worth it.

"Sure, I was safer, but at what price?" I thought.

I was very introspective at that time. Luckily, a steady stream of customers was tapping on the taxicab window. They drew me out of my thoughts and pulled me back into the moment. Sure, the passengers could be hard on me, but, at times, I was harder. So I tried to stay busy.

I cruised for passengers near Vancouver's hot spots. Train stations, airports, and stadiums were great for business. When there weren't any arrivals or games, I stayed close to the nightclubs and restaurants. The people were often weird, but I needed the business. One thing I learned while driving a taxi is that you can't always count on people acting the way they look.

One time, a client asked me to take her to White Rock, which was at least a fifty-dollar fare. I was very excited. As she was about to get in, she saw that my taxi didn't have a cassette player. She left to find one that did. On a wintry evening, I picked up a very muscular man. I took him to Westside. The ride was more difficult than usual. By the time we got to the area where he lived, it was icy and hailing. I slowly proceeded down the road. No one else was out on the street.

"Stop!" the passenger demanded. "Or you're going to die."

I didn't want to die, so I stopped. It was cold. I was scared and shaking, wondering how I was going to get out of this one.

He leaned in closer to me and said, "You can't go any further. It's just too slippery. I'll pay you here, and you can turn around before it gets worse."

"Thank God," I muttered.

"Excuse me?" he asked.

"Nothing, sir," I said. "Thank you."

I felt like a fool for judging him for what he looked like.

I thought, "I, of all people, should have known better."

At about three o'clock in the morning, the time that the ladies who worked the streets finished their business and headed home, I picked up a very beautiful young woman. She looked like she might have been a teenager. I drove her to her destination. She hopped out of the car and asked me to wait for her.

"I'll be back in fifteen to twenty minutes, all right?" she said.

"Okay," I said.

I watched her walk into the building. But, after forty minutes of waiting, I saw her come out of the building. She was shuffling and looked drugged.

"Here," she said, handing me an address written on a piece of paper. "Take me home."

I was very upset because she didn't even apologize for being late. At the same time, I felt sorry for her. I wanted to say something to her. I wanted her to see how much opportunity there was for her and she didn't have to live this way. So I did.

"Shut up!" she yelled. "You're just a taxi driver. What do you know about life? My life is none of your business. Just drive."

I realized I had made a mistake, so I didn't say anything until I asked her for the fare. She only paid me ten dollars.

I earned around one hundred dollars a day, including tips. The pay looked good until I factored in my time and effort. I worked at least twelve hard hours a day. In addition to arguing with passengers, I had to argue with other taxi drivers. It was a very competitive business. We often fought over passengers. The hours and the arguing wore me down.

* * *

I had been in touch with Yahya, and I had even visited him. He tried to convince me to move to Montreal and study with him for the medical exams.

"It's impossible to pass," I said.

"Almost impossible, but still possible," he said. "If you're not going to move out here and study with me, at least look for a job in the medical field. Maybe it'll remind you of your dream and why you left your family and Afghanistan behind in the first place. At the very least, it'll boost your confidence."

He had a point. So, I decided to quit and find work doing anything in the medical field. I applied for various jobs, but nobody wanted to hire a foreigner who only spoke broken English.

"Thank you for the opportunity," I said repeatedly as another door closed in my face.

"You ought to look into an LPN program," someone said just before she closed a door on me. "It would give you time to work on your English and keep your skills fresh."

She shut one door, and I opened another.

"Enter a licensed practical nursing program?" I thought.

I tried to picture it. I thought about my days in the hospital in Afghanistan. I remembered just how hard the nurses worked. Not only did they work long hours, but those hours were filled with taking care of all the dirty work. I decided to apply. At least I'd be in the medical field. I mailed an application to one of the community colleges. They accepted me. With the help of a student loan, I joined the program.

The bookwork was a breeze. The practical work was a pain. After years of being the one who gives orders, it took a lot of time to get used to being the one who follows orders, especially since they came from nurses. But I did get used to it. I even started to enjoy the patients, despite the fact I was cleaning up their bowel movement mishaps and taking care of other "not so fun" aspects of nursing.

I really liked my elderly patients, and I will never forget some of the people I met on my nursing home rotation. One of those patients was Mr. Dyer. Mr. Dyer had severe pneumonia when I first met with him. With multiple medical afflictions, only one of which was an amputated leg, his overall health was fairly debilitated. Out of everyone I met, he had a few good excuses to be unpleasant.

Despite his physical condition, Mr. Dyer was always in a delightful mood and filled with adventurous life stories. I enjoyed taking care of him. By the end of the rotation, when it was time for me to leave, I realized I was going to miss him terribly. He had touched something in me. I had learned the value of making the most of what I had. From then on, I looked forward to completing the coursework and entering the medical field as an LPN. I was excited.

Then my sister-in-law called from Afghanistan. A group of men who knew my family and knew I was living in the West had kidnapped my eldest brother, Abdul Mateen. The abductors demanded one million Afghan rupees, around five thousand dollars, in exchange for his life. My brother's wife pleaded with me to save him.

"Mohammad," she said, "you're the only one who can do anything. You have to save him. What will happen to us? Oh, God, what will happen to my children?"

She broke down crying. On the outside, I told her that everything was going to be okay. On the inside, I panicked.

I hung up the phone and cried out, "Why? Why me, God? What did I do?"

My sister-in-law didn't have to beg. I was going to do anything that I could to secure my brother's freedom. There was only one way I could afford to pay for my brother's release. I dropped out of school the next day, walked to the bank, and sent the rest of my student loan money to my family. The next week and a half went by very slowly. I finally received a phone call.

"Thank you, Mohammad," Abdul Mateen whispered through the phone.

"No need," I said. "No need."

Chapter Seventeen:
Almost Impossible

This latest blow set me back financially and emotionally. It depleted me of all the money I had saved and all the hope I had of ever getting into the medical field. At that point, it seemed to me that my medical career was over. I had given up my life in Afghanistan with my family and friends for nothing.

Father's voice returned to my head.

"I told you it'd never happen. You'll never amount to anything. It's impossible!"

I felt like a boy again, but something was different. Without an opponent to fight, I didn't have any fight in me. I gave up on medicine and searched for the best-paying job I could find. If I was lucky, it would be one I enjoyed.

Once again, I didn't have to look hard. A friend of a friend of mine named Murray Logan was a resident housing supervisor at the University of British Columbia. He gave me a part-time position from eleven o'clock at night to seven o'clock in the morning. My job was to help the dormitory residents with typical issues like lost keys and guest registration. I also dealt with building maintenance issues. The job paid nine dollars an hour, and it gave me medical and dental coverage. I quickly earned a full-time position, giving me annual vacation and sick leave. I couldn't believe my luck.

In addition to those benefits, I actually enjoyed interacting with the college students. They were educated, engaging, and more accepting of my differences. Even my English improved. I was making more money at an easier job. I was happy.

* * *

"You're not happy, Mohammad," Nadir said. "What about your dreams?"

"Trust me," I said, "I'm happy. Besides, unless I want to start over completely and get a general degree in science and then a degree in medicine, which, by the way, would be really expensive, I have no hope of getting into a residency."

"What about the exams you mentioned?" Nadir asked.

"The exams?" I asked. "Oh, there's no way I can pass those."

"How do you know that?" he asked.

"No one I know has passed them," I said. "It's supposed to be almost impossible."

"Since when has 'almost impossible' ever stopped you, Mohammad?" my brother asked. "You need to stop lying to yourself. You are not happy. You are depressed. And I know you. If you aren't working toward a goal, then nothing in life is right."

"Well, you don't know me very well then. I am perfectly happy working this job," I said. "Even if I did save the money, it'd be hard enough for me to remember everything I learned in our own language. Imagine how much harder the exam will be in English?"

"Mohammad, look, the hard part is over," Nadir said. "You're there. You're right there. Don't give up now. It's not what you do. This job is not the goal. It's a path to your goal, but you didn't leave everything you love behind to hand out keys and pick up after a bunch of people as they make their dreams come true."

His words stayed with me long after our conversation ended. I tried to imagine my life without medicine. I tried to imagine myself at the same job in five years. I couldn't do it. I had come too far to let a pricey exam or, rather, a few pricey exams stand in my way.

The problem with comfort is that it encourages complacency. It was easier for me to work toward my goal when all the odds were against me. As soon as I had a comfortable income, work surroundings, and place to live, I avoided discomfort. When I lived in Afghanistan and India, I thought my tests and difficulties were the problem. In reality, they were my reason to fight.

* * *

"Hey, you! Where are you from?" a man asked as he walked up to my table.

He had been sitting in the booth across from me. His jeans and jacket were soiled with dirt. His dark brown hair looked as if it hadn't been washed or brushed for days, maybe weeks. I dreaded getting into a conversation with him, but I figured he'd go away faster if I answered his questions.

"I'm from Afghanistan," I said.

"Go away. Just go away," I begged him inside my head.

"Afghanistan?" he asked, wrinkling up his face and exposing his rotting teeth. "Where in the world is that? And what are you doing here?"

By this time, from his smell and swagger, I could tell he was drunk, so I chose my words carefully.

"There is a war in my country, so I came here for safety," I replied.

"Safety!" he said. "Ha! If there were a war in my country, I'd be fighting. Why aren't you fighting for your country?"

My eyes burned. My throat closed. I certainly wasn't expecting that question. I swallowed the emotion that rose in my throat and said, "I am fighting. This is my fight: to come here, live my dream, and help my family back home. One day, I will help them rebuild."

My own words made me sick. They weren't false, but they were a lie.

"So what's this dream that's so important?" he asked.

"I'm going to be a doctor," I said.

"Ha!" he exclaimed. "You? A doctor?" He started laughing. "How's that going to help anyone?"

"I told you," I said, raising my voice. "I'm going to help my family. When I can, I will go back and help my people."

He didn't care. He didn't even listen. He just laughed. He laughed all the way out of the diner. But he had given me a reason to fight.

I remember that stranger, especially his face and his words, to this day. If I had known when he approached me that he was about to give me a reason to fight, I would have thanked him from the beginning of our conversation.

"Who was that man?" I asked God that night as I prayed. I hadn't prayed in a long time, but I was drawn, like a flower to the sun, to turn my face to God and ask for guidance.

"Was he an angel? Was that a sign? What do I do?"

Not too long after that encounter, my temporary position at the university ended. I received an opportunity to move to Montreal and study for the medical exams. I took it.

As an unemployed worker, the Canadian government paid me 60 percent of my salary, about one thousand dollars a month. That money helped out with my living expenses so I didn't need to work.

"Yahya," I said into the phone. "Guess what, buddy?"

"What?" he asked.

"I'm here," I replied.

"No way!" he said.

"Yes. And I'm ready to study. I'm ready to beat those exams," I promised.

The next day, I went to the Kaplan Education Center, where I met Yahya and another guy from Afghanistan named Farid. Farid was three years ahead of us at the University of Afghanistan. Both Yahya and Farid had taken the Canadian evaluation exam for foreign graduates as well as the Educational Commission for Foreign Medical Graduates (ECFMG) exam. They had both failed these exams several times, but they hadn't given up yet.

"We'll make it this time," Yahya said to Farid.

"Definitely," Farid said. "The Kaplan course is all we need."

Their enthusiasm was encouraging, but the fact they had both failed was not, especially since Yahya had been one of the brightest students in our medical school. He'd been first in our class, and he had remained one of the top three people in the entire medical school throughout the seven years we were there. It was only with his help that I'd passed medical school at all.

Every morning, I left the apartment and went straight to the library, where I studied until noon. I left to eat lunch and then went on to the Kaplan Center, where I stayed from one thirty to nine o'clock.

On my first day at the Kaplan Center, I didn't know where to start. Yahya suggested I start with psychiatry because he had more experience in that area and would be able to help me. I opened the book and found a list of terms that I had never seen before.

"Hey, buddy, what is this?" I asked Yahya. "Is this a joke?"

"No," he said. "Don't worry. It gets better."

He continued to assure me that, once I learned the new terms, it would get easier, but I had a hard time believing him. After all, he himself had failed the exam. My confidence faded with each page I turned. I almost cried right there in that room. I started to wonder if I had traded the best job I had ever had in Canada for a mailbox filled with failure notices.

"Perhaps," I started thinking, "I should have settled for comfort and complacency."

While some of the diseases, such as depression, were common in Afghanistan, others, such as the various personality disorders and addiction disorders, were not recognized in my country. I had been through seven years of medical school and never even heard of Wernicke's encephalopathy, a disorder of the brain associated with alcoholism.

Nevertheless, I pushed thoughts of inferiority to the background and tackled the new terms one at a time. I studied for more than twelve hours a day, and I started to notice improvements. Although I didn't feel ready for the exam, I went ahead and registered for the clinical portion of the ECFMG, which was scheduled for six months after the day I had started studying.

The Kaplan Education Center was located on the second floor of a very nice building in downtown Montreal. Yahya, Farid, and I took our study breaks at a coffee shop on the first floor. There, we met with other foreign graduates and discussed our struggles as foreigners and our frustrations with the tests.

Six months passed quickly. In January 1991, it was time to sit for the exam. I was nervous. I hadn't slept well in the past couple days. I knew I had to get a good night's sleep on the night before the exam, so I took ten milligrams of Valium. It made me a little too relaxed.

I had set the alarm clock for six o'clock to give myself a chance to take it easy and get to the exam center in plenty of time. Instead, I slept right through the beeps.

"Oh, crap!" I exclaimed when I woke up as I noticed it was a little too light outside. I looked at the clock. "Seven forty-five!? What?!"

The exam started in fifteen minutes, so I skipped my morning shave and jumped into and out of a cold shower. My hair was still wet when I slammed the apartment door behind me. My eyes scanned the street for a taxi as I ran in the direction that I needed to go. After a few minutes, I got a taxi and rode to the exam. I hoped that, when I got there, they would allow me to take the test. I arrived just as the administrator was shutting the doors.

"Good morning," I said to a lady as I squeezed in between the gap in the doors.

"Humph," she said, looking at my hair strangely. "You're lucky you got here when you did. If you had been another second later, these doors would have been closed."

I went in, sat down, and ran my fingers through my hair.

"No wonder she stared at me like that," I thought to myself. "My hair is frozen into icicles!"

The test started. I opened the book, took one look at the first question, and swore to myself, "Crap!"

I glanced at a few more questions.

"What the heck is this? These questions are impossible to answer!" I thought as I turned each page.

I took a deep breath and decided that all I could do was give each question my best answer and not worry. The more questions I answered, the angrier I grew. I couldn't believe that I was sitting there, unprepared. When I finished the exam, I went to the coffee shop, where I met up with Yahya, Farid, and our other friends.

"What a joke," one of the men said. "It's a scam. It's got to be a scam. They just want our money, so they let us take this test, knowing we'll fail."

"It may not be a scam, but it sure is a waste of money," I said. "There's no way I passed."

I was 99 percent certain I had failed and 100 percent pissed off at myself for leaving Vancouver for the slight chance of achieving my dream.

"Damn it!" I said to nobody in particular.

Yahya and Farid tried to reassure me, but they couldn't hide their fear of their own failure. The doubt in their eyes contrasted with their words of encouragement.

The days after the exam went by slowly. No matter how sure I was that I had failed, a ray of hope flickered despite my gloomy predictions. I decided I would continue to study until my fears were confirmed.

A month later, when I went to the mailbox to receive the usual stack of bills, I found a results letter.

"Okay, buddy," I said aloud, "this is it."

I wanted to get the worst over. I ripped into the envelope, unfolded the piece of paper, and read it.

"What? There's no way!" I thought.

I couldn't believe it. I scrutinized the letter. I was sure I had made a mistake. But I hadn't. I had passed the exam. Unfortunately, both Farid and Yahya, who were way ahead of me in preparation, had failed.

"At least I know that it can be done," Yahya said.

"Yeah, now we know it's not a scam," Farid added.

I was upset for them, but I was happy for myself at the same time. For the first time since I moved to Canada, I knew without a doubt that I could become a physician. I just had a lot more exams to pass.

In March 1992, I took the Canadian Evaluating Exam and passed that one, too. Yahya and Farid failed the exam, but my success again encouraged them. They pushed me to keep going. I spent the rest of the year studying and then sitting for exams.

In June 1992, I took the first portion of the ECFMG. I passed. Shortly after that I took the first portion of the United States Medical Licensing Exam (USMLE). I passed. Toward the end of 1992, I took the first two parts of the Federal Licensing Exam (FLEX) exam and the first part of the Licentiate of the Medical Council of Canada (LMCC). I passed all of them.

I was also broke. The exams were very expensive. Each one cost a few hundred dollars. When I lost my unemployment benefits, I went to the welfare office to see if I was eligible for any money. They enrolled me and gave me five hundred dollars a month.

In another few months, I had ended up pulling off a perfect passing streak. I thought the worst was over, but it was time for another test, residency applications.

* * *

I applied to all of the residency programs in Canada. I wasn't invited to interview for a single position. Despite the blow, I decided to send some applications to the United States. I got some help with my résumé, but, no matter how good that looked, I still needed letters of recommendation. I couldn't get a letter from my university in Afghanistan because all the schools and universities there were shut down. I asked a few people whom I knew in Vancouver and Montreal to write letters for me. My former boss at Mac's Store, Moc, wrote one. My cousin Daud Nassery, who'd known me as an intern in Afghanistan and had been my attending physician, wrote one. And an Afghan doctor practicing pediatrics in New Jersey wrote one.

I sent three hundred applications to various hospitals and universities across the United States and waited. After a couple weeks, the rejection letters started coming. Day after day, they trickled in. And, day after day, I held my breath as I read repeatedly that I would not be invited to interview. After I had heard from almost all of the three hundred, I gave up.

* * *

One cold Tuesday in February 1993, I received a letter that surprised me. It was an invitation to an interview. I couldn't believe it. My heart raced. I realized I had finally been given a break. All I needed and wanted was a break. As I read the letter further, I saw that they wanted me to interview that very day at Frankfort Hospital in Philadelphia. My spirits were dashed as quickly as they had risen. I felt as if I had been tripped in a soccer match and had fallen on my back. The wind was knocked out of my body.

For a minute, I didn't know what to do. Then I decided to call the hospital right away. I reached one of the secretaries.

"I'm sorry, sir," she said, "but there aren't any more interview slots. I can't reschedule you."

"But it's not my fault," I said. "How could I be there on the same day that I receive the letter? That would be … that's impossible."

I continued to plead with her. I couldn't let her hang up the phone. That was my one break, and I wasn't about to let it slip between my fingers.

"Sir, there's nothing I can do," she said.

"No, don't …"

I drew a deep breath and sighed. Words failed me. I couldn't even say good-bye. I took the phone from my ear. I was about to hang up when I heard her voice again.

"Sir—" she started. "Sir?"

"Yes," I said quickly as I put the receiver to my ear, "I'm here."

"You might want to try our other campus. Maybe they have an interview left. Would you like the number?" she asked.

"Yes! Yes, I'd like the number. Thank you very much," I said.

I quickly grabbed a pen, scribbled a series of numbers next to a name, and called.

"Well, there is one interview left," the secretary said. "It's on the sixteenth of February. Do you think you could make it?"

"Yes, I can make it. I'll be there!" I said.

I hung up the phone and looked up the numbers I needed to make a reservation for the train and one night's stay at a small bed and breakfast close to the hospital.

The morning of the interview, I awoke a total wreck. I walked into the breakfast area and greeted my host. He asked me the purpose of my stay.

"I have an interview," I said at first. But then I started to ramble. "It's a job interview. I sent out hundreds of applications, and I only got this one interview. Three hundred applications in the United States, not including the ones in Canada. So this is it. This is my one shot."

"That explains why you look so nervous," he said. "You should relax. Here, have a bite to eat. Don't worry. I have a feeling you'll do just fine."

* * *

I arrived at the hospital and discovered that three other people were interviewing for the same position. We each had different interviewers. Mine asked me about disease, diagnosis, and procedures.

"If someone paged you about a patient lying on the floor, what would you do?" she asked.

"I would find the patient and turn him on his side so he doesn't vomit or aspirate. Then I would ..." I continued with the appropriate treatment.

I was so nervous that I wasn't sure if I had gotten everything exactly right. When I finished, she smiled and complimented my English skills. I relaxed.

By the end of the interview, I must have felt either really comfortable or really desperate.

Before I left her office, I blurted out, "I'm afraid you don't understand how much this job means to me or how much it hurts me to lose a profession like medicine. If I get back into my profession, it would be the best thing that's ever happened to me and my family. Please give me a chance. Please, you've got to give me this job."

She said she'd do her best for me. Another person or two would be interviewing me, and they would all have a say in the selection.

I returned to the waiting area with the other interviewees. After fifteen or twenty minutes, a very nice lady came and asked me to follow her to her office.

She got straight to the point. She asked, "I see you are a Muslim. Would you be able to work with women?"

"Well, yeah, I love women," I answered honestly.

She tried to ask me her next question, but she started to giggle. Her giggle turned into laughter. She laughed so much that she couldn't stop. I thought it was good that I had made her laugh, but I really didn't mean to be funny. We continued our interview with the usual round of questions.

Once again, I felt I had to express how important it was for me to get back into the medical field. She also told me that she would try her best and the interviewers would meet and decide after everyone was interviewed.

I returned again to the waiting room. Three people approached me: the two ladies with whom I had just interviewed and a man who identified himself as the program director.

He said, "Congratulations, Mohammad, you've made quite an impression here. I'd like to offer you a position."

"As a resident?" I asked.

"Well, yes, of course," he said.

"Are you sure?" I asked.

"Absolutely, we'll have you saving lives in no time," he said.

* * *

I packed a single suitcase and left Canada for Philadelphia in May 1993.

* * *

"Excuse me," a woman says, interrupting my lunch. "Dr. Alikhail?"

"Yes," I say.

"Do you recognize me?" she asks.

I stare at her. Something seems familiar, but I just can't place her.

"I guess I look a little different now," she says.

"I'm sorry," I say. "I just don't recognize you. Do I know you?"

"I'm the woman who drowned, the one you saved," she says.

"Oh my! It's good to see you again!" I say, standing up and shaking her hand.

"Well, thank you. I have something I'd like to give you," she said.

"Yes?" I ask.

She reaches into a bag and pulls out a plaque that thanks me for my dedication.

"I hear you worked for two-and-a-half hours to keep me alive and you are the one who never gave up hope. I was so lucky to have you."

"Well," I say to her, "A long time ago, I learned not to give up hope."

"I'm grateful to you and the lessons that made you who you are. Thank you," she says.

She hands me the plaque and embraces me.

"I'm the lucky one," I say. "Thank you."

Afterword

Years after I'd completed my residency, my oldest daughter, Laima, looked up at the night sky in South Carolina with wonder as it spread above her. On the surface, I shared in her excitement, but, in my heart, I longed to show her Saikanda. There, the stars don't just dazzle. They blaze. To her, Saikanda is another world. Children like my friend Anwar aren't best friends; they are the sad faces of a foreign land, faces she knows only from television.

Whenever I can, I tell stories about my adventures in Afghanistan to my four daughters.

"Daddy, when can we go?" they ask me.

"I'm not quite sure," I say. "One day."

Then I tell them one of their favorite stories. "Did I tell you about the time that I bought a *saira* in Kabul and took it to Anwar?"

"As you know, one of my favorite hobbies was to find different ways to cheer up my best friend ..." I begin.

And then I tell them of our adventures.

* * *

In 1991, before I moved to Montreal to study for the medical exams, I went to Pakistan to visit Mother and Abdul Mateen, my oldest brother. They were living in a refugee camp for my village. When I visited them, I also found some of my childhood friends.

As I was walking one day, I noticed a familiar-looking man with a dark face behind a grey beard. His worn clothes barely clung to his thin frame. My heart jumped at seeing him, but my mind didn't make the connection right away.

"Mohammad!" the man said.

I knew the voice.

"Anwar!" I yelled.

Not only did I learn that day that Anwar was alive, I learned he was married. But I learned that none of his six children had lived to see their first birthday. I couldn't imagine burying six infants. All of them had died from dehydration. Their little bodies had been racked with nausea and vomiting, which the microbes living in the muddy drinking water caused.

Despite this devastating loss, Anwar was upbeat and encouraging.

"I told you that you'd make it," Anwar said to me as we said good-bye.

"I haven't made it yet," I reminded him. "There's still a long way to go."

"But you will, Mohammad. Trust me," he said.

"Yeah, I will," I said.

"And I'll help make everything better," I promised to myself.

I looked at the conditions around me and wondered how anyone could be happy there. The refugee camp was crowded and filthy. It was one hundred to one hundred ten degrees outside. Everyone lived in tents with no electricity and no means of keeping cool. Because of the lack of food, jobs, and money, the young, beautiful girls resorted to prostitution in order to feed their families. The very people who were there to protect the refugees often took what little money they did have.

I was embarrassed to say good-bye to my family and leave them behind for another life that was so completely different from and better than theirs. As I boarded the plane to return to the United States, I prayed for the opportunity to live with all my family and friends again someday in Saikanda.

* * *

I returned to Pakistan in 1995. The situation had worsened. People sifted through garbage to find food scraps. Mothers sat in the streets with their children, hoping someone would take pity and toss them some rupees. Hardly anyone had proper clothing for the harsh winter.

I never found Anwar or his wife. To this day, I hold on to the hope that they got out somehow and started a new life somewhere. Only one thing stopped me from sinking into depression again. I met the woman who would become my wife.

* * *

In 2006, my wife received a call that melted my certainty that leaving Afghanistan had been my destiny, the right thing to do, into a puddle of doubt. Walking out of the airport, finding a taxi, and getting to my cousin's address had been so easy. Even my wife didn't have the heart to give me the news. She told a colleague and good friend of mine, and he delivered the news to me.

"Mohammad," he said, "this is really hard for me to tell you, but I've got some information about your family."

"Yeah? What is it?" I asked.

His words puzzled me.

"What could he possibly know that I don't know?" I wondered as I straightened up and prepared for the worst.

"Your brother Nasir killed himself," he said.

"What?" I said.

"Your niece Susan called today. She talked to your wife. She called me because she just didn't know how to tell you," he said.

"How?" I asked.

I swallowed the emotions that threatened to take control away from my rational adult to the little boy who hurt inside of me

"Pills," he said. "I'm so sorry. Are you okay?"

"Thank you," I said. "I'll be all right."

After hearing the news that had come from a refugee camp in Peshawar, Pakistan, I slumped into a chair in the dining room, where I would spend the next half hour, my mind and heart warring with each other.

The table and eight chairs in the dining room are one of the last remnants of my life of struggle. That furniture has seen to the comfort and service of many polite guests and four growing girls, one of whom is only just learning to sit at the table respectfully. The table's scratches and bruises identify it as an outcast among our furniture. My wife had handpicked many pieces for the house we had just built.

My heart felt out of place, longing to be in the refugee camp with my family and wanting to share in this time of sorrow. My mind was straining in its efforts to justify my affluence in the face of the horror my family was experiencing.

With a mental ladle, I stirred the still and quiet memories that had settled over the years, lifting them from their slumber at the bottom of my mind to the surface, where I could sift through them and recall the ones I needed. I stared at the images I had just recalled, sequenced them together, and reminded myself that my life was as it was meant to be. It had to be. As determined as I was to leave Afghanistan, ultimately, fate's hand was also on the wheel. At the very least, it was responsible for some of the road signs that had taken me that far.

I rose from the chair and wondered how to go about interrupting my daughters' play to explain to them that their uncle, a man they had only known by name, was dead. Then I even wondered if I should bother. At the very least, I would spare them the details. What they know of suicide is not what I know of suicide.

Perhaps Laima, the oldest one, has drawn the common, naïve conclusion that suicide only happens to sad or strange people, the odd ones who don't quite fit in. What I know is that, during times of war, nobody fits in.

Outside times of war, the problems persist. War is a pebble tossed into a pond. The disturbance war causes, like the liquid tentacles of a deadly squid, ripple out and carry with them the harsh realities that mass killing and fear affect generation after generation, long after the last gun's barrels have corroded.

Nasir's death is just one example. His two children are yet another example. They are poor, illiterate, and discarded. The first, they cannot help. The second, they haven't the means to overcome. The third is unfortunate because it says more about the world than the children themselves. The struggle between mind and heart ended. Heart won. The little boy inside sobbed.

* * *

Although I had started a new life in the West, I always kept an ear tuned in to the news from Afghanistan. I celebrated in February 1989 when I heard that the last of the Soviets were withdrawing from my country. But stories of mass civil unrest soon followed that news. Afghans were not happy with President Mohammad Najibullah.

In 1992, the *mujahideen* took control of Kabul from Najibullah, but they continued to fight amongst each other for control over the country. Divided and unable to unite and run the nation cooperatively, the stronger warlords fought for and gained control over various regions of Afghanistan. At the same time, the Taliban, a Sunni Islamist fundamentalist movement, organized and started fighting the splintered, unorganized *mujahideen* groups, who were already weakened from fighting each other. After four years and the loss of fifty thousand lives, the Taliban gained control of 90 percent of the country. They ruled from 1996 until American-led coalition forces overthrew them in 2001.

Since then, Afghanistan has been all over the media. I no longer have to point out to people where Afghanistan is on the globe because of the prevalence of maps on the television evening news and in the newspaper. Unfortunately, that knowledge is often mixed with myth.

* * *

A second-grader raised her hand during one of the talks I gave to my daughter's Montessori school.

"Why do people from Afghanistan hate the United States?" she asked.

My heart sank.

"Where did she get that idea?" I wondered.

"The people of Afghanistan do not hate the United States," I answered. "I'm from Afghanistan, and I love this country. In fact, almost every one I know in my country loves the United States and wants to move here."

She looked puzzled and said, "Oh."

Even adults are influenced to make generalizations and assumptions about people who are not so different from them. On the day the United States started bombing Afghanistan, I stood in the hospital and watched the news. A woman I regard as extremely intelligent was standing next to me.

"I hope they level that country to the ground," she said coldly.

"Why?" I asked her.

"That's where bin Laden is from. Afghanistan," she said.

I was amazed that, despite her education, she knew very little about her country's affairs.

"Osama bin Laden is not from Afghanistan," I said. "I am."

She turned to look at me.

"Bin Laden is from Saudi Arabia," I replied. "This is not the fight of the people of Afghanistan and my country. My family and my friends do not deserve to be leveled to the ground."

Unfortunately, she was not alone in her mind-set. I watched the news that night as an interviewer asked a "man on the street" how he felt about going to war.

He said, smiling, "I say, 'Let's go kick some butt!'"

* * *

I've lived through war. No matter which side you are on, there is nothing to smile about. I've lived with the killing, bombardment, suffering, invasion, poverty, and depression. It's horrible to be the victim. And I believe it's horrible to be the oppressor. Nobody should have to live through war, especially today. There are other ways to solve our problems and other ways to fight the diseases that fuel war.

I hope this book somehow conveys the feelings of the suffering, abandonment, and poverty of those whose countries are caught in war situations. I want others to understand what it's like so that, at the very least, they don't smile when they talk about going to war and don't want their country to level another country to dust.

Though my family members have been in Pakistan for much of the conflict, they weren't spared the hardships that the conflict in Afghanistan caused. I've already mentioned the deplorable conditions of poverty in which my family lives. Though they may be better off where they are, I feel sorry for them and the millions of my countrymen living as refugees in Pakistan, Iran, India, and other neighboring countries. I hope that they and I can eventually return to the land we love.

I haven't seen my family in Pakistan since 1995. Both of my parents died as refugees living in Pakistan. I have a sister there with eight children. I have four brothers. Each has small children. None works. I send them five hundred dollars a month to split among themselves. My nieces and nephews, the future of our world, are growing up illiterate and uneducated. They are little victims of a war that the big powers of the world created.

Despite the ups and downs of the last twenty-two years away from Afghanistan, I am grateful for the opportunity to fulfill my dreams here in the United States. Some of my friends from Afghanistan are here. While not everyone has fulfilled the dreams he or she came with, dreams do change.

Yahya is practicing medicine in Los Angeles, where he lives with his wife and three children. My friend Akbar, the taxi driver who studied engineering, lives in San Francisco and works as a taxi driver. He was reunited with his wife and children when they finally received their visas. He had lived in the United States by himself for six years. Shafi also lives in the United States. He decided not to pursue medicine after being released from prison and making it to the United States. He started out by sitting on street corners and selling single roses. Rose by rose, he saved enough money to start a construction company that is now thriving.

Despite our successes, many of us still dream of going back to Afghanistan and making a difference. I dream of rebuilding Saikanda. My brother Nadir went back recently.

"The entire country is in bad shape," he said. "They could really use you, especially in Saikanda. It's a ghost town. At most, there are twenty families there. One thing hasn't changed though."

"What's that?" I asked.

"The stars," he replied.

* * *

Despite recent efforts to transform the health care system, statistically, my home country remains among the worst in the world. In 2000, the World Health Organization ranked Afghanistan one hundred seventy-three out of one hundred ninety-one countries. Life expectancy at birth was only forty-two years.

It would be easy to blame my country's poor health statistics on recent history, including twenty years of civil unrest, war, Soviet occupation, drought, the oppressive rule of the Taliban, and a recent incursion by an American-led coalition, but data shows that Afghanistan's health problems date back at least fifty years. A further probe into Afghanistan's history reveals that the country has endured multiple invasions and a long history of oppression and poor health. The British Empire invaded three times. Genghis Khan invaded in the thirteenth century, destroying the country at large. Many centuries before that, around 330 bc, Alexander the Great spent four years in war there.

* * *

I started my life journey in Afghanistan, and I want to finish it there. I want to see my friend Anwar again. I want to walk with him among the proud mountains of Afghanistan and sleep beneath the stars that sparkle in her skies.

My dreams of returning to Afghanistan reach beyond reconnecting with my friends. I want to use my education to save lives. I want to teach people about health and sanitation. I want to show them simple steps to clean drinking water that will save their children from dying. I want to build a small free clinic and invite my American colleagues to work there.

Still, my dreams go further. I look forward to freedom and social progress. I look forward to the day when a woman runs Afghanistan, all of our children have access to an education, and our country, once again, becomes the center of tourism in Asia. I look forward to the day when soldiers or the *mujahideen* don't stop us and force us to answer questions about our personal and religious beliefs. I look forward to the day when we can walk through our home country and feel at home.

Made in the USA
Lexington, KY
01 December 2013